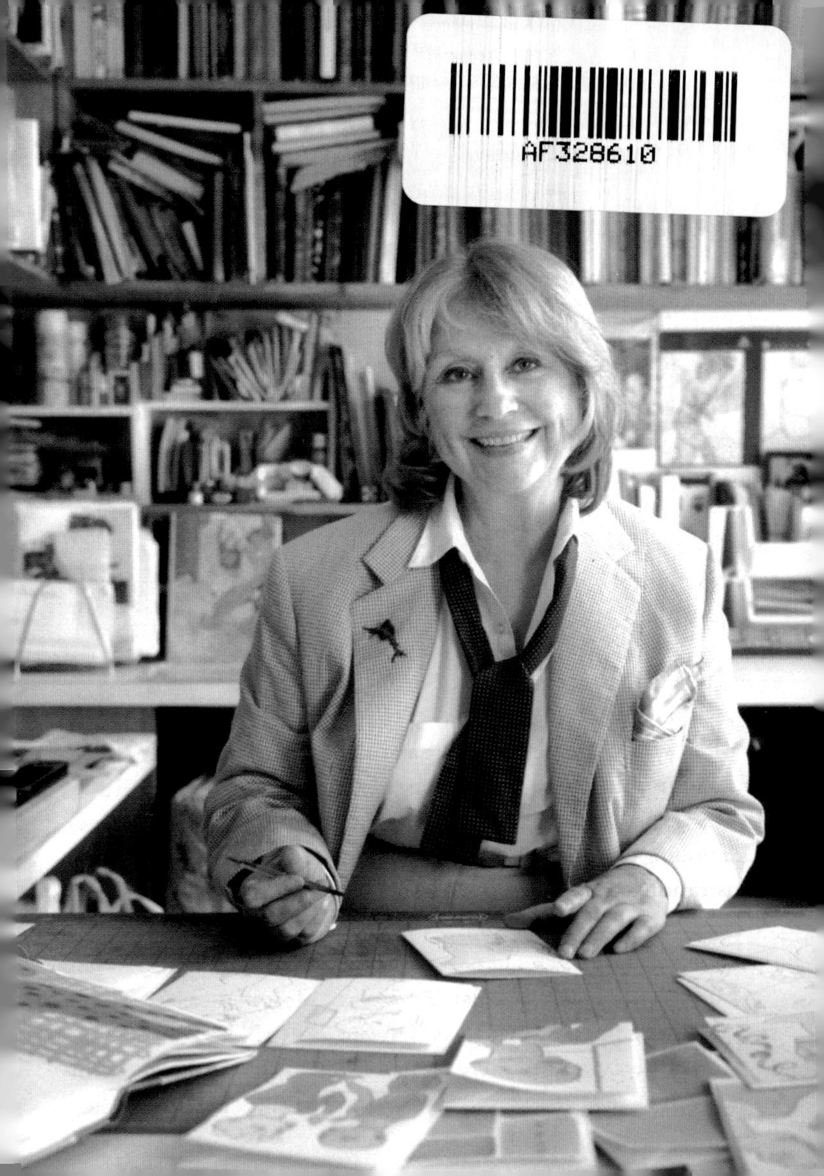

AF328610

Eichenberg, Jacob Landau and a string of other "originals." I also loved rhythm and blues and Latin music and I loved to dance. Creating art and dancing were my passions.

Q What made you decide to become an illustrator?

A Well, in the back of my mind I didn't think I would become an illustrator. I was sure I'd be in advertising and perhaps own an agency. I also didn't think I was that talented. So I was very surprised when I started to pursue being an illustrator and liking the challenge. While in school I worked summers as a fashion illustrator for buying offices.

Q Tell us about your first job out of school.

A During the last few months in school I put together a mailing list of art directors in book publishing, made a woodcut, printed 100 signed prints and mailed them out. Within a week I got my first job— a book cover for Doubleday. After graduation I got a job three days a week doing colorings for a textile company and the other two days I took my book around to art directors. On the weekend I worked on any job I happened to get. I also entered the Society of Illustrators annual show and won an award for a series of monotypes. Art directors saw that work and that led to other assignments.

Q How did you arrive at your unique style?

A This is an interesting question. I never consciously tried to have a "style." In the last semester of my senior year I had an upsetting

2003

STUDENT ILLUSTRATORS ANNUAL

SPONSORED BY 3x3 MAGAZINE

HONORING

Barbara Nessim

EDUCATOR : ILLUSTRATOR OF THE YEAR

PUBLISHER

Charles Hively

ART DIRECTOR & DESIGNER

Sarah Munt

COPY EDITOR

Kate Lane

PHOTOGRAPHY BY

Katarzyna Gruda

INTERN

Devon Spencer Smith

SPECIAL THANKS TO

Darlene Smidian

Holly Neubeck

PRINTED IN FRANCE BY

Imprimerie Toscane

PUBLISHED IN 2004 BY

3x3 MAGAZINE, 244 FIFTH AVENUE, SUITE F269, NEW YORK, NEW YORK 10001

COPYRIGHT 2004 ISBN 0-9755158-0-2

Barbara Nessim is an artist, illustrator, teacher and innovator—a self-taught computer artist whose work is equally at home on the cover of a magazine as it is hanging on a gallery wall. Mastering a series of computer programs when no other artist was even remotely interested in the new-fangled computer, Barbara led the way and pioneered the world of computer art and opened up a whole new category of illustration. In addition to expanding the use of the computer in the commerical world, Barbara has also enjoyed the notoriety of having her art exhibited at the Louvre. A forever curious pathfinder, Barbara has also found time to teach and served for the past 12 years as the Chair of the Illustration Department at Parsons School of Design in New York. We honor her dedication to both art, design and education as our first recipient of this award given to outstanding educator/illustrators. — THE PUBLISHER

Q Tell us about your early schooling and influences?

A The High School of Industrial Art (now the High School of Art and Design) was my first introduction to an "official art school." The daily commute from the Bronx gave me independence as well as opening the door to an urban landscape full of interest—Manhattan. Continuing on to Pratt Institute I entered the Department of Illustration and Fine Art. I was much more interested in the commercial side of the department since I wanted to focus on doing art to make a living which I felt gave me the independence I was looking for. My views were unpopular in my class. Most of the class was interested in fine art. I had very definite ideas of who I was and what I wanted. My influences were David Stone Martin, Richard Lindner, Bob Gill, Robert Weaver, Tomi Ungerer, Thomas B. Allen, Fritz experience and the only thing that made the pain go away was doing small, narrative oil paintings. They were very colorful, figurative, and had lots of symbols representing the stories of my life. I did not

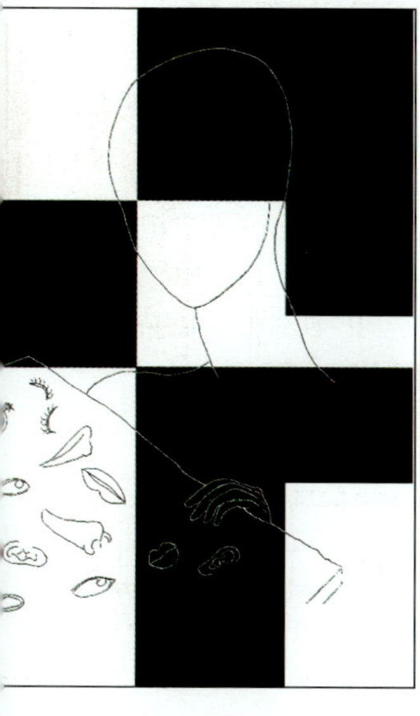

show them to anyone. They were totally for my own well-being. By accident, one of my teachers saw the paintings and asked me about them. After a long conversation I came to realize that these paintings were truly "me" and that is how I started to recognize the beginning of my "style." During my school years I always had a sketchbook, but since I had this revelation I started to keep a different kind of sketchbook. In these 6" x 9" books I continued my secret drawings. The more drawings I did the more they developed and the more they became mine. I still keep these sketchbooks and do about three or four a year. They keep me connected to my subconscious.

Q Have you always been preoccupied with line drawings?

A During my entire career I have continued to experiment with many mediums, I enjoy developing new techniques and mastering them. Doing line drawings was just one way of working. I've always felt that drawing is one of the most important skills an artist has, besides the all-important thinking.

Q Are your drawings done from life, dreams, personal experiences, events in your life or are they spontaneous results of ink on paper?

A They are all of the above. I love to draw from life. When I'm not drawing from life I will start with a line, anywhere, and that line will suggest something and then I continue until a drawing is finished.

Sometimes I have an idea before I start, but most of the time I just let it happen and I am always surprised by the result. When I work for a publication or an agency I have to consider and be aware of so many aspects of the art. I am there to visually express my interpretation as well as satisfy the idea behind the story, satisfy the editor, the art director and of course to provide an interesting and visually informative aspect to the reader. I am always aware that I am a "service." When I work for myself I want to be totally free to wander. I enjoy both ends of the spectrum.

Q There's a timeless quality to your work, why do you think this is so?

A I try to keep the figures very neutral. I accomplish this by clothing my figures in leotards and eliminating any hairstyle on the women and men. Then you can't pin an era to any of the pictures.

Q What prompted you to explore the digital world?

A To make a long story short: In 1980 I was invited to MIT in Boston to learn how to use the computers they were developing for graphics. I was then to lecture on the work I produced. I was never able to afford the two months time it would take to go to Boston, but I was so intrigued with the idea that I actively looked for a computer here in New York. Fortunately Time Incorporated had a new "secret" program they were experimenting with that was a precursor to the internet. I was invited to be an artist-in-residence and was allowed to work on their computers from 5:00 PM to 9:00 AM during the week. Over a period of two years. I taught myself how to use the computer which resulted in a body of work that I could show. Since this was so new, there was immediate interest in the work.

Q Are you using the computer to draw or as a reproduction device?

A Over the last 24 years I've used the computer in so many ways. When you are learning something new you are always experimenting. One of the major challenges is not creating the art, but how you show it. You have to think about the end result as you create the art. I have

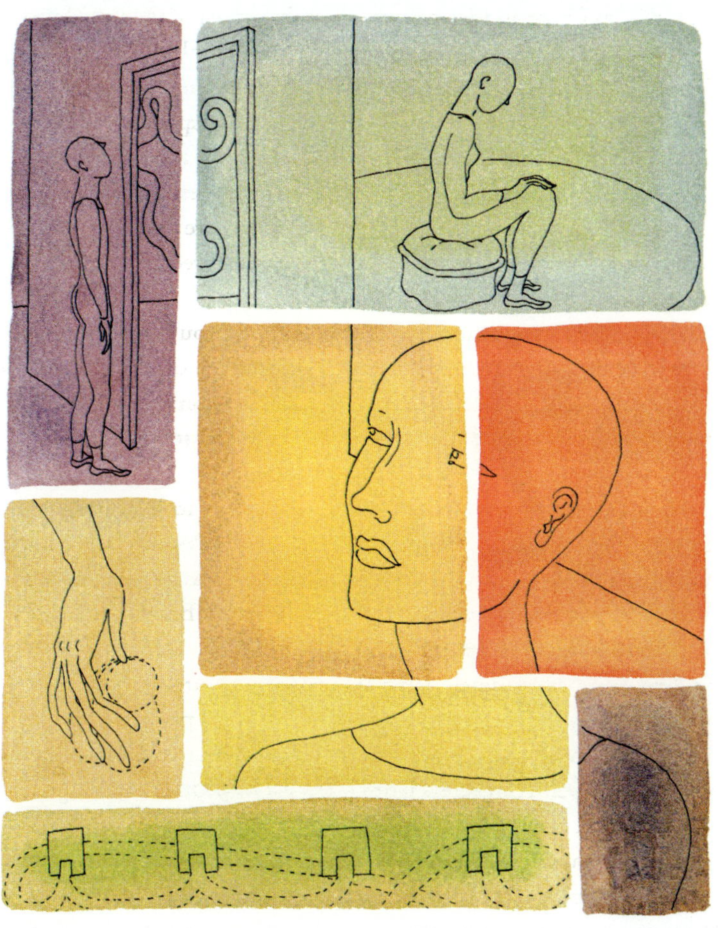

done 35mm slides; CIBA-chromes; videos; inkjet prints; Polaroids, as well as hand-colored, tiled, larger artworks; mini-sketchbooks that the viewer/participant assembles; 3D Stereo-pair works; very large modular works; prints on stretched canvas; and "randomly"

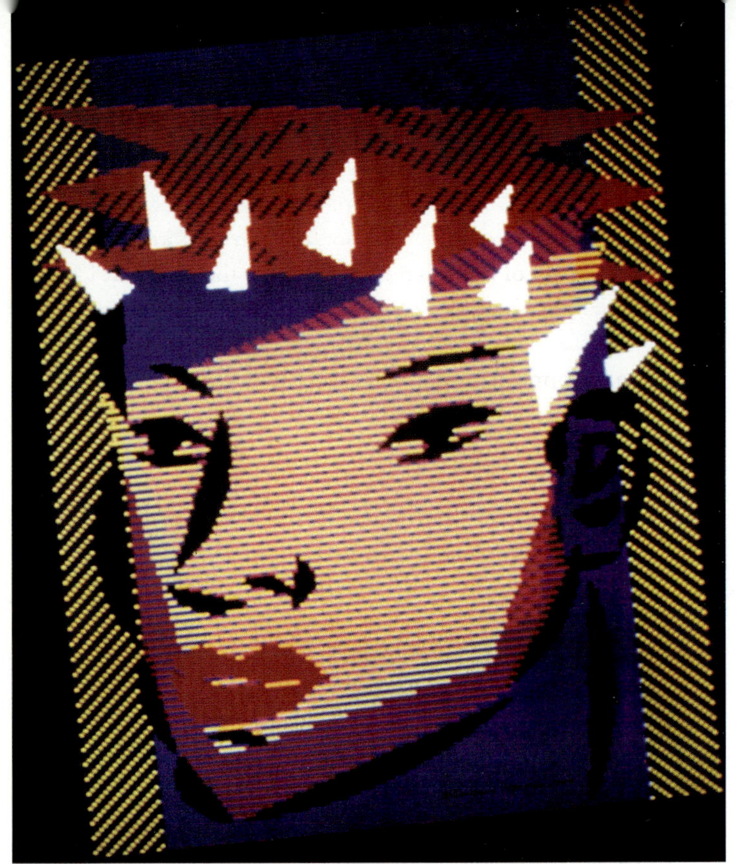

moving software art shown on a wall-mounted monitor. I am always
thinking of new ways to show my art.

Q Why do you think so few artists have followed you into the digital area?

A Because it is challenging to be constantly learning something new all
the time. It is a bottomless pit. But that said, using new cutting edge
tools and media opens up the creative process to new possibilities
you cannot achieve using traditional methods. I am very curious and

I find the investigation so interesting.

Q What do you think about the current state of illustration?

A This is a big complicated question and I will try to address it simply.
We are in the midst of a revolution. As in every revolution, change is
challenging the "norm." Most people have an aversion to change.
That goes for artists as well. Traditional illustrators are not getting
the same amount of work they have gotten in the past. But I believe
in every change there is an opportunity as large as the change taking
place. One has the chance of exploring new markets. Illustrators
now have the opportunity to learn and get comfortable with type and
design as well as learn about digital photography. That way they can
provide complete design services for a client, not simply the illustration. Or using technology, a moving image can be used in so many
ways on web sites or TV. And there is also licensing art for products.
The world is always changing and we have to change with it.

Q What part do you believe a good business mind plays in being a
successful illustrator?

A I think a major part. Good business, in my mind, means a lot of
things. Having a good understanding of people, being open to new
opportunities even if they may seem strange in the beginning, not
being afraid to venture into new areas. You may still continue doing
illustration while augmenting your income doing other kinds of
creative work such as lecturing about your art or teaching.

Q As the Chair of Parson's Illustration Department what have you seen
as the key differences in the graduates who have become successful
illustrators? Is it motivation? Skill set? Or luck?

A A few have become successful illustrators, some have found niche
markets, but all are benefiting from their digital skills. Graduates
have told me that because of their education here they have been able
to get full time jobs in many different areas. Whether it's video
games, toy design, fashion design, film, television graphics, web

design, graphic design or self-publishing comic books and graphic novels. Some decide to go into new areas that are art related while others have ventured into completely different fields. For instance a recent grad was hired to illustrate a project for MTV. He was asked to do still frames which evolved into a 35-second animation using Adobe AfterEffects. They had originally planned to hire someone else to animate his art but because he was so versatile he made ten times the amount he would have. That's what I mean about seeing new opportunities. Luck may play a part in everything in life, but don't count on it.

Q As a teacher how have you helped students develop a personal style?

A When I teach I have always tried to identify what is unique in their work and ideas. I tell them "there is only one of me and there is only one of you." That is where each one's uniqueness begins. One should not force a style. If it is meant to be, then you will have a unique style. I always believe that if you love drawing and doing your art, a style will develop by just doing and being aware of your production. That means looking at a body of work and "reading" the message you are producing.

Q Any final words for graduates?

A Staying connected to your classmates after graduation and forming friendships based on creative interests is key. Sharing your work with others and seeking mutual crits from and with friends is also important. That way you will continue to grow.

For the complete interview log-on to www.3x3mag.com

2003

Student Illustrators Annual

JUDGES

Kolea Baker
SEATTLE

Marc Burckhardt
AUSTIN

Seymour Chwast
NEW YORK

Ivan Cottrell
LONDON

Amy Demas
NEW YORK

Richard May
LONDON

Gary Taxali
TORONTO

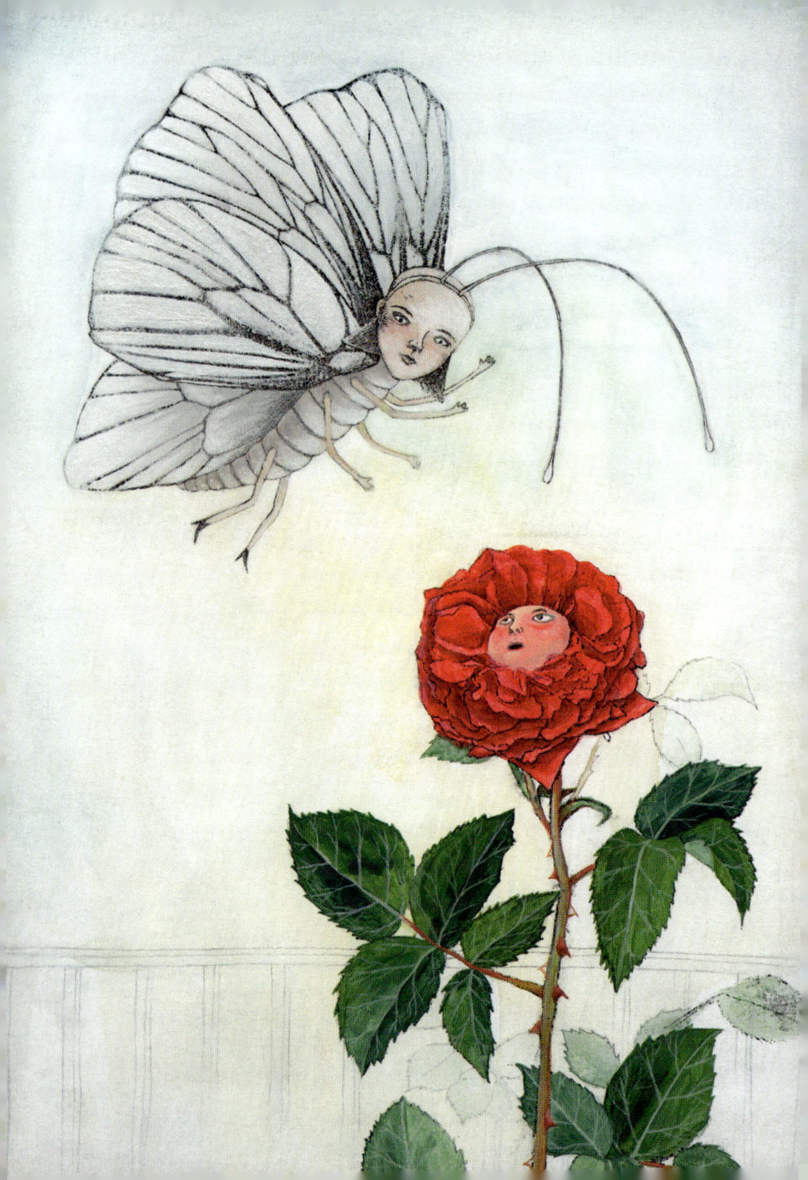

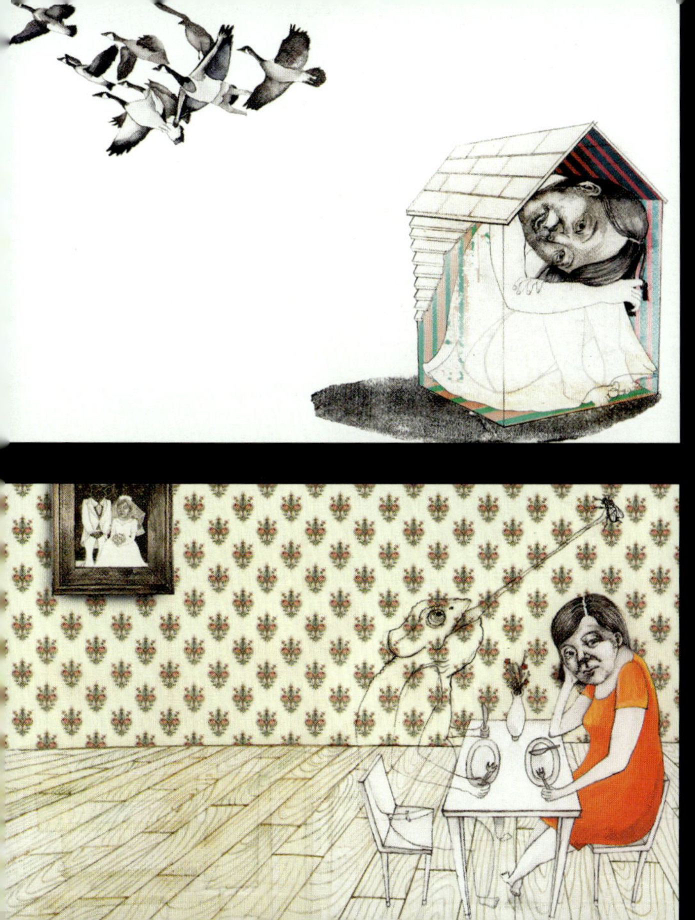

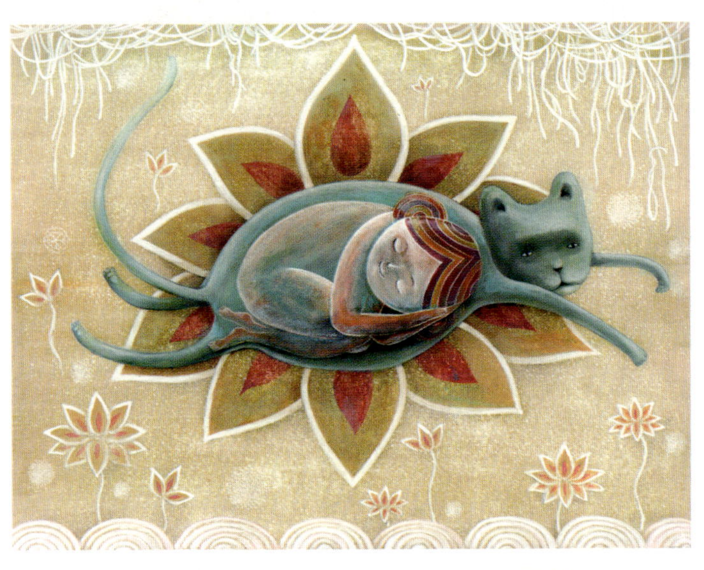

WOOJUNG AHN : woojungahn@hotmail.com
Instructor David Sandlin, School of Visual Arts, New York

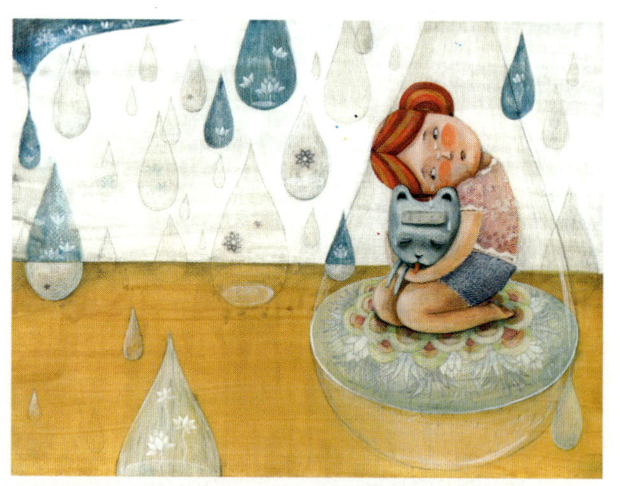

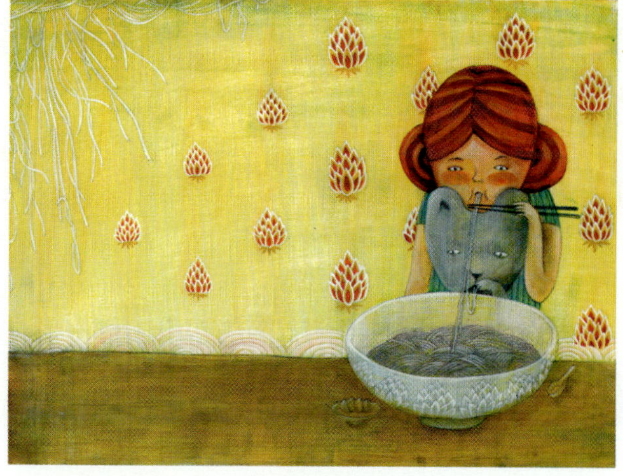

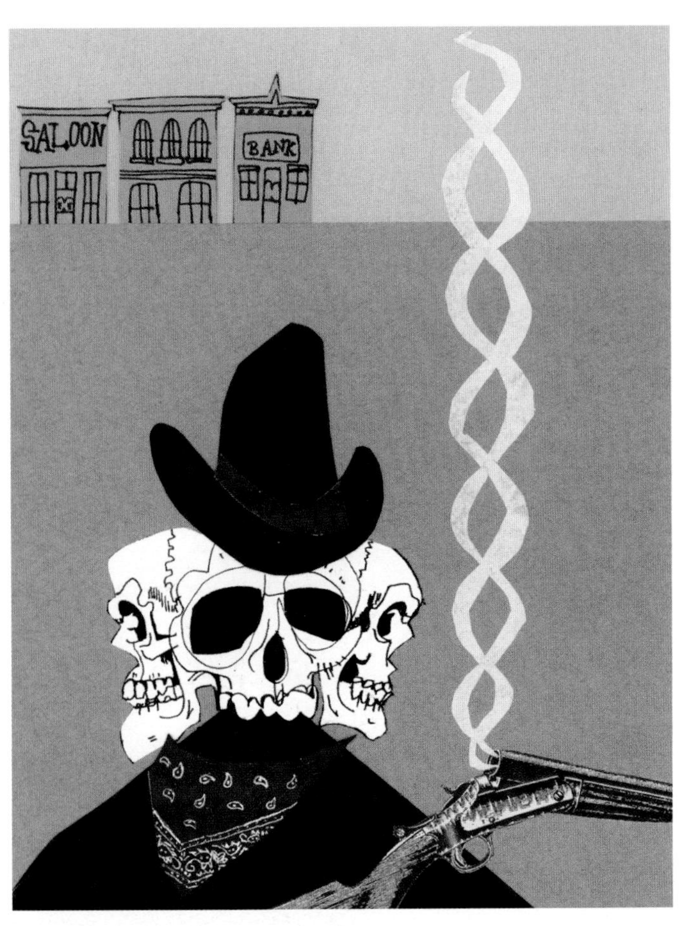

JASHAR AWAN : JQHA@hotmail.com
Instructor Jordin Isip, Pratt Institute, New York

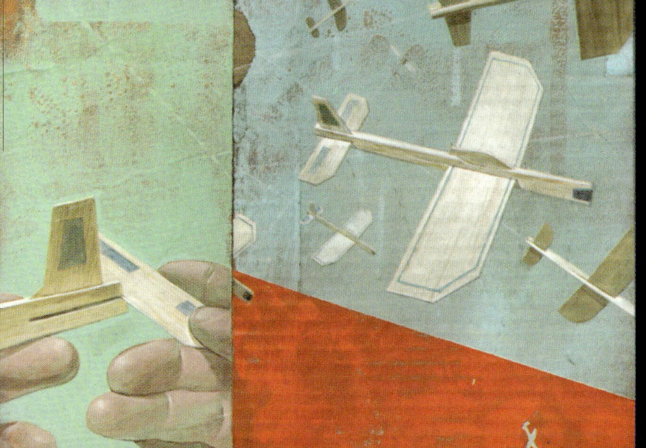

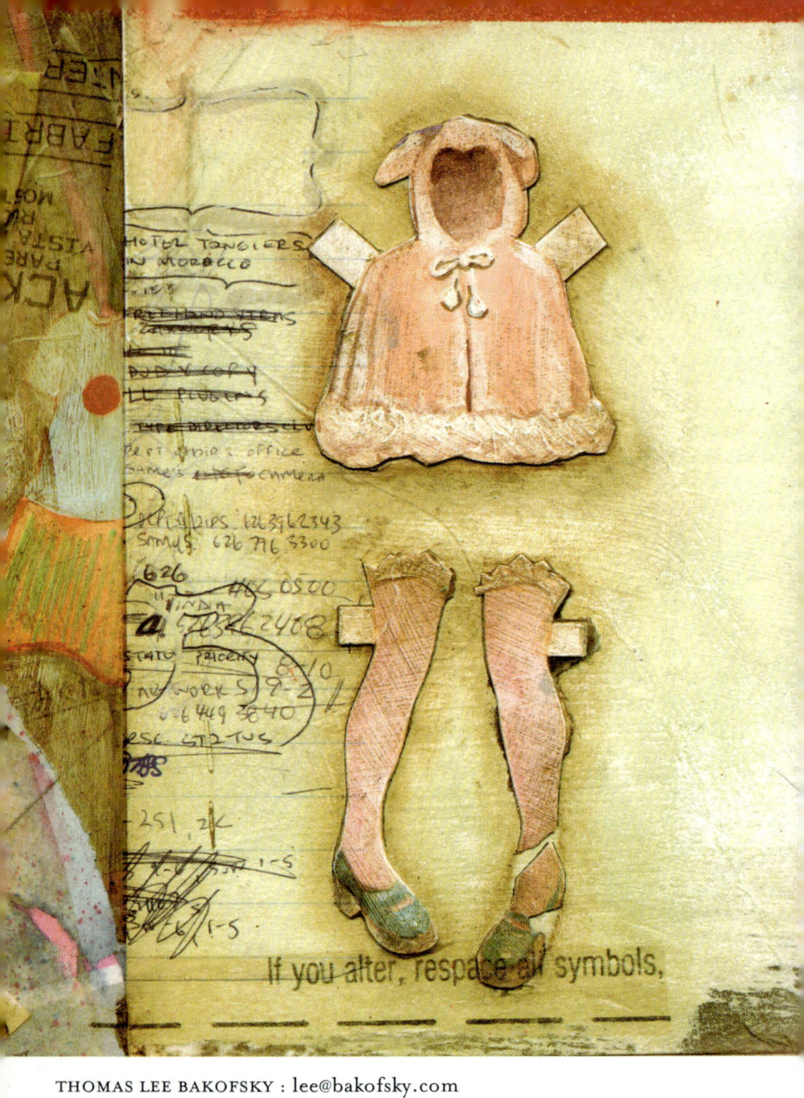

THOMAS LEE BAKOFSKY : lee@bakofsky.com
Instructor Jim Salvati, Art Center, California

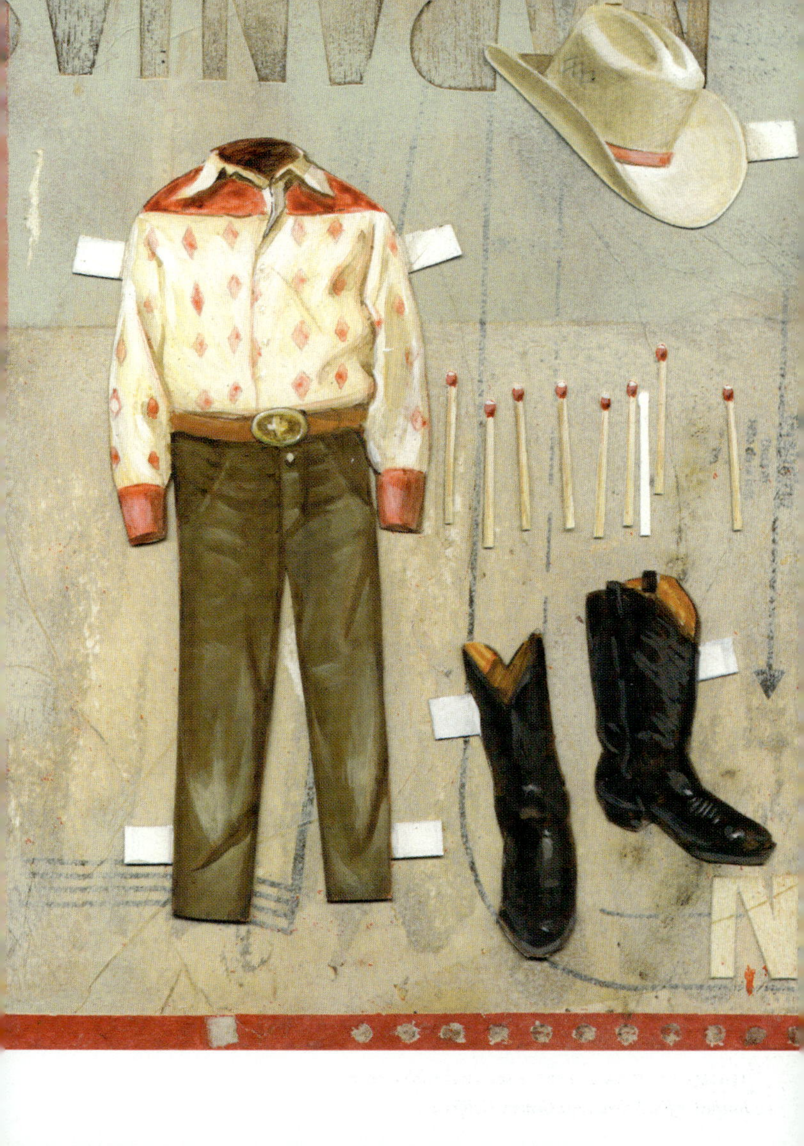

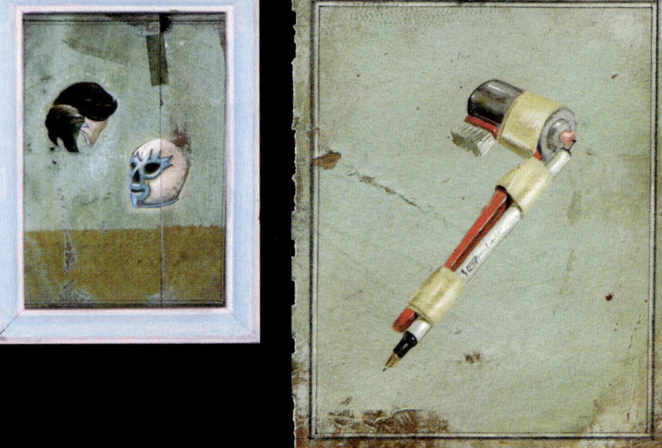

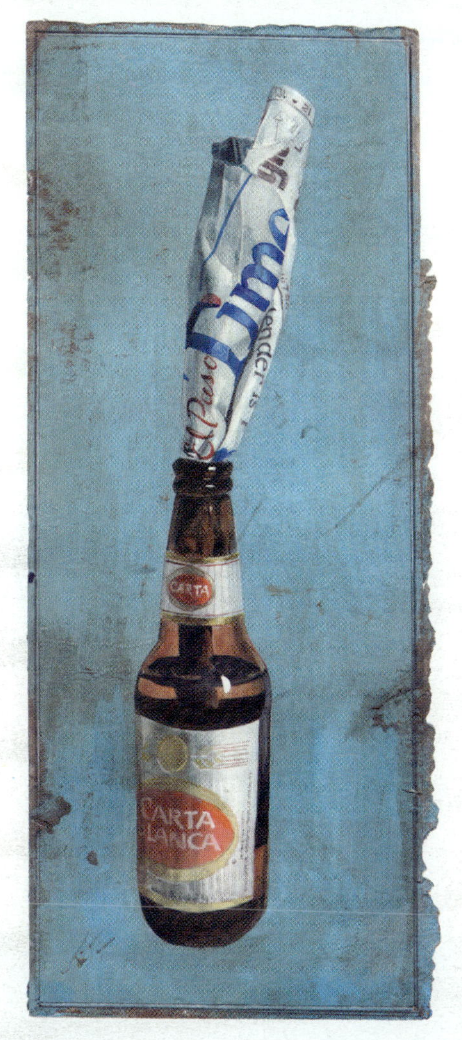
Lime
El Paso
ender
CARTA
CARTA
LANCA

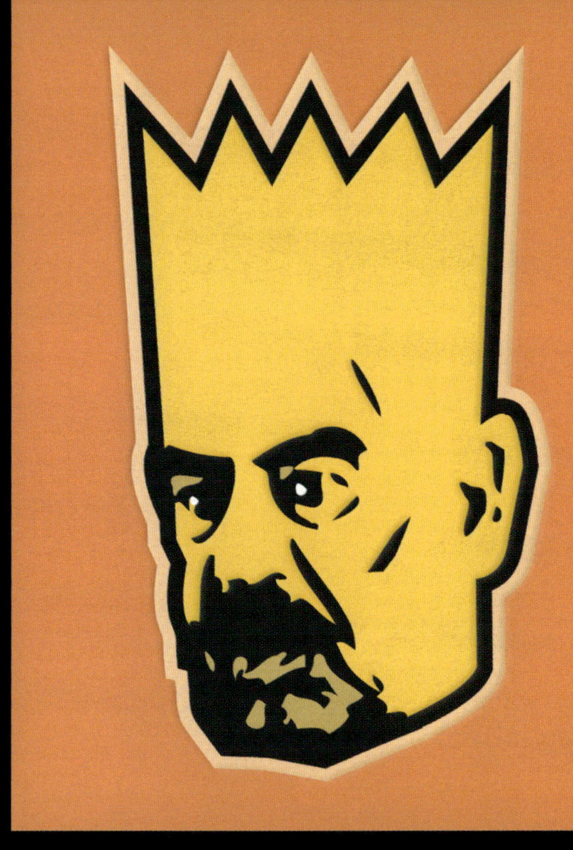

THOMAS LEE BAKOFSKY : lee@bakofsky.com
Instructor Jim Salvati, Art Center, California

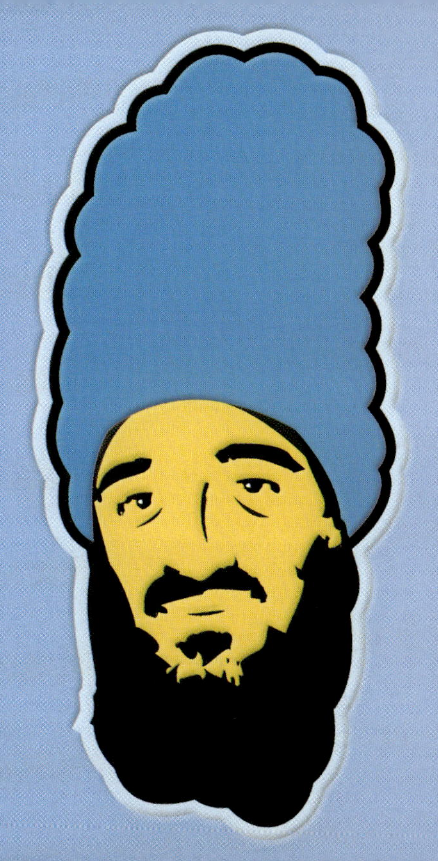

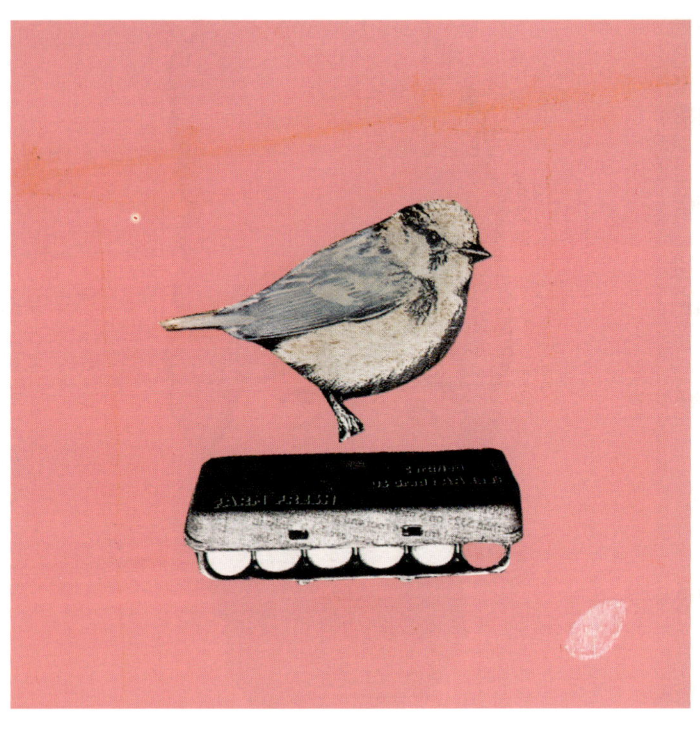

CRYSTAL BARLOW : barlow32@yahoo.com
Instructor Tom Garrett, Minneapolis College of Art & Design, Minnesota

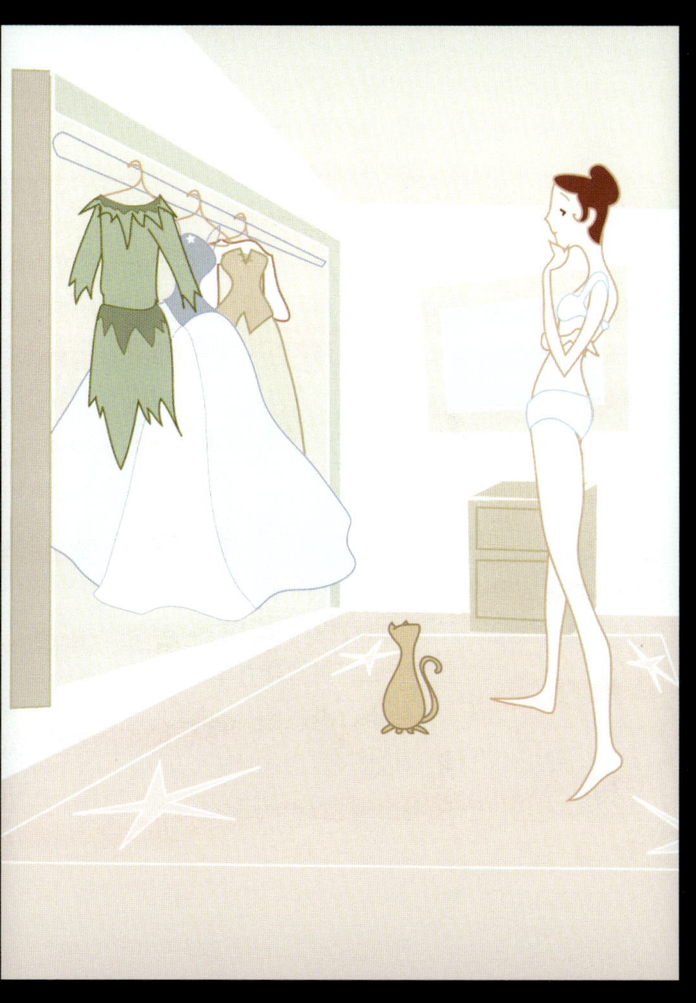

SARA BUTCHER : dreamflier@dreamsenses.com

Instructor Peter Lochner, Minneapolis College of Art & Design, Minnesota

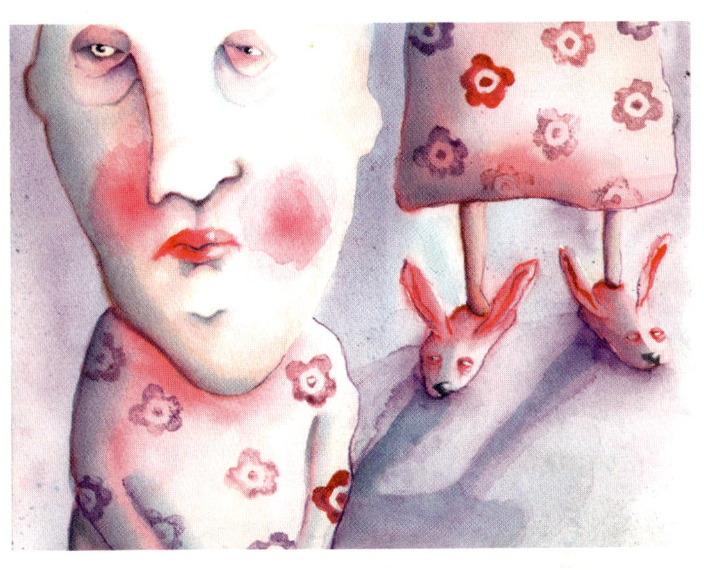

ALICE CARTER : wwonderlandd@hotmail.com
Ontario College of Art + Design, Toronto, Canada

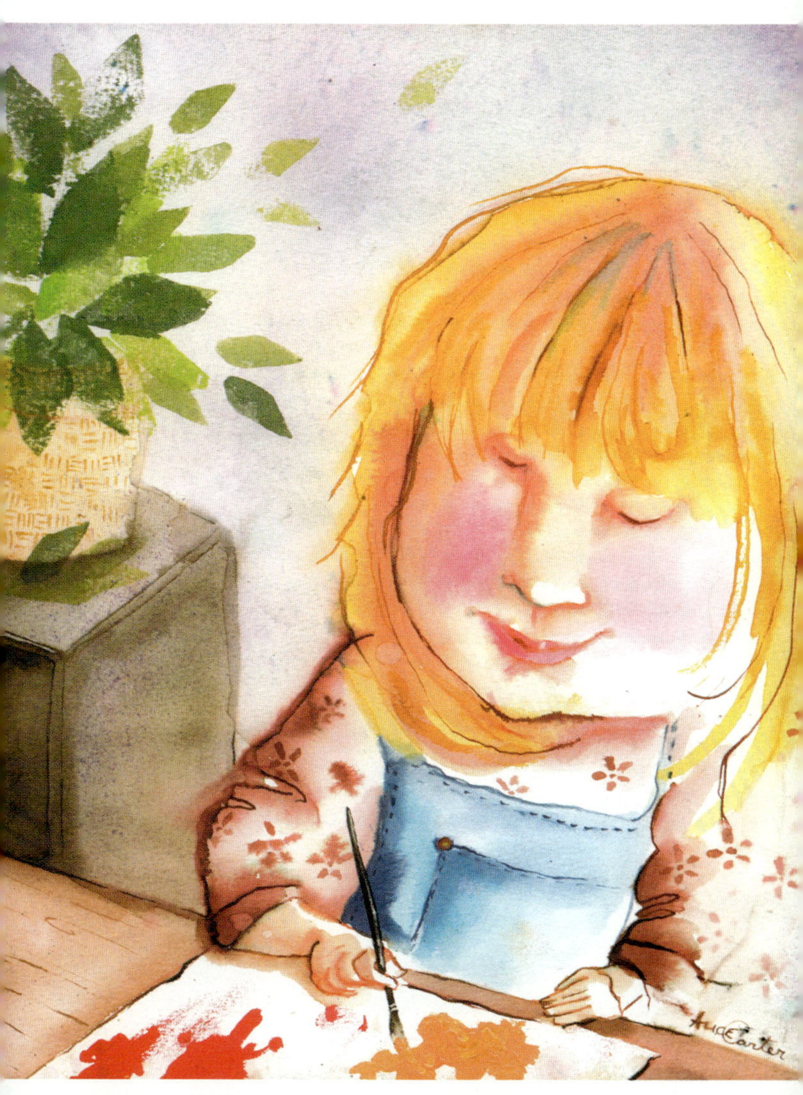

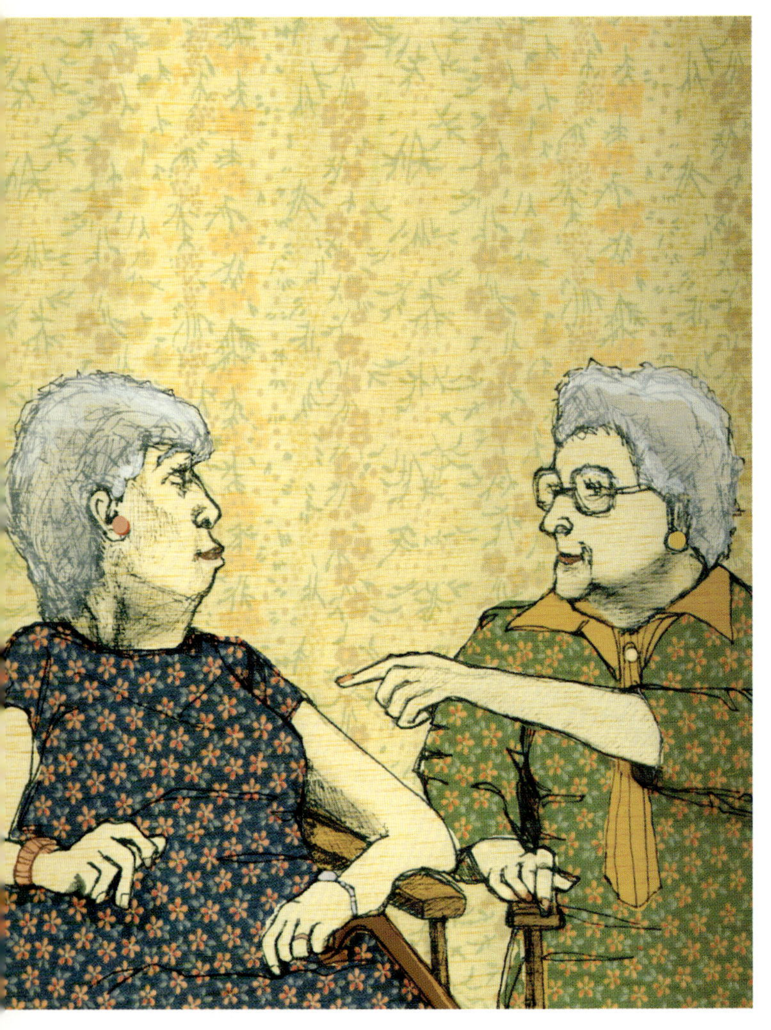

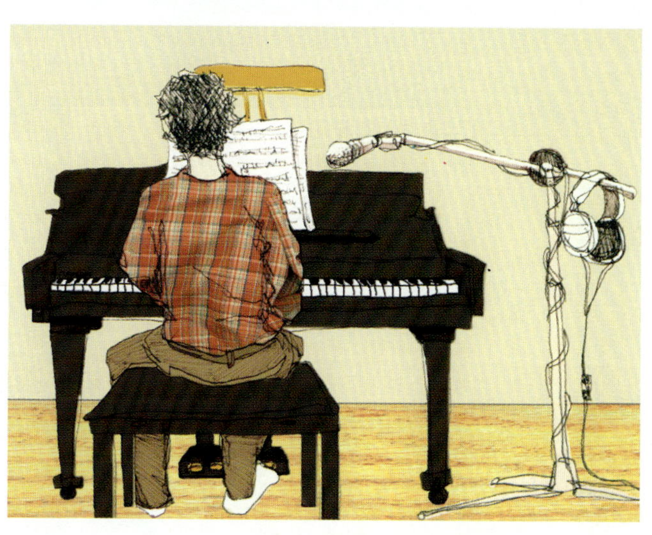

LAUREN CASTILLO : info@laurencastillo.com
Instructor Marshall Arisman, School of Visual Arts, New York

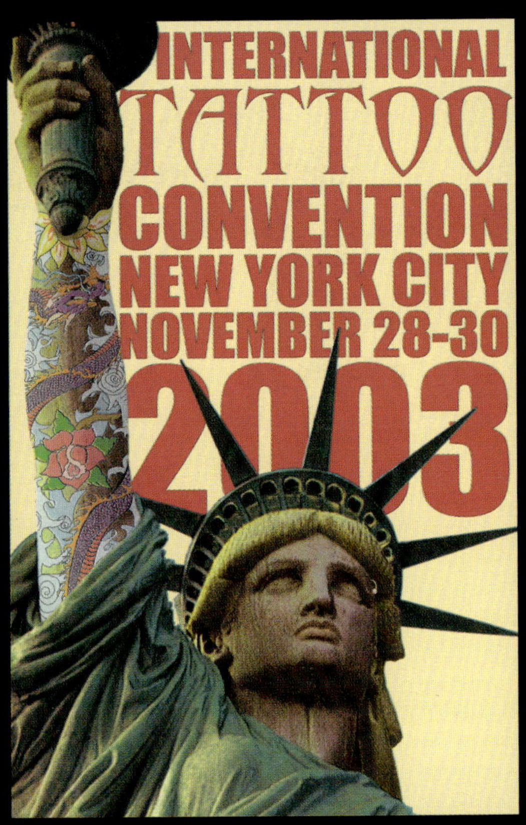

above: DERREK COSS : d13sk8s@hotmail.com
Instructor Rebecca Bradley, The Art Institute of Boston, Massachusetts

right: ANDY DAVIES : andyroberdavies@yahoo.com
Instructor Andrew Selby, Loughborough University, Leicestershire, United Kingdom

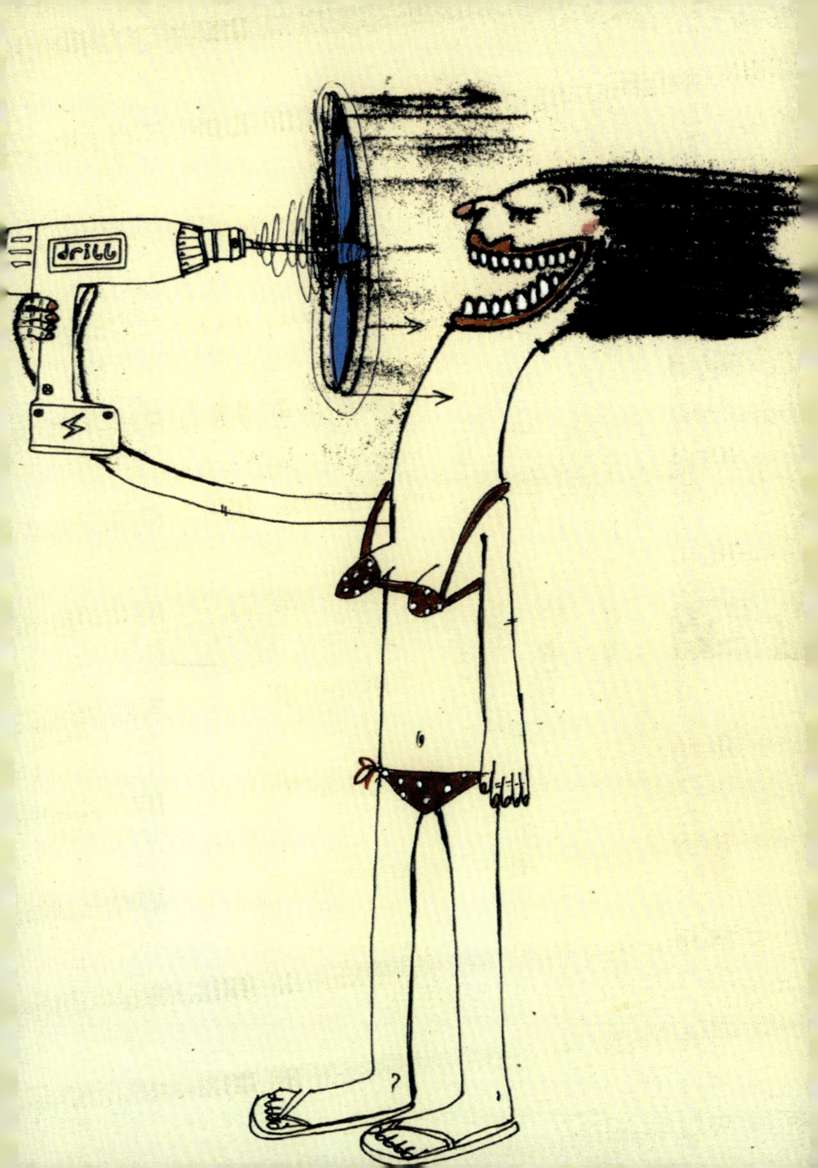
drill

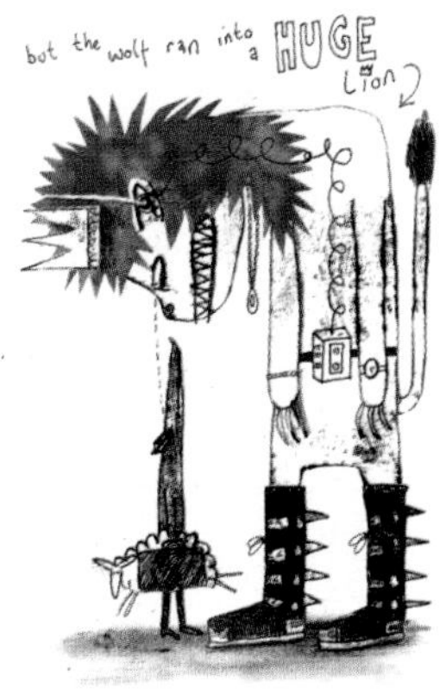

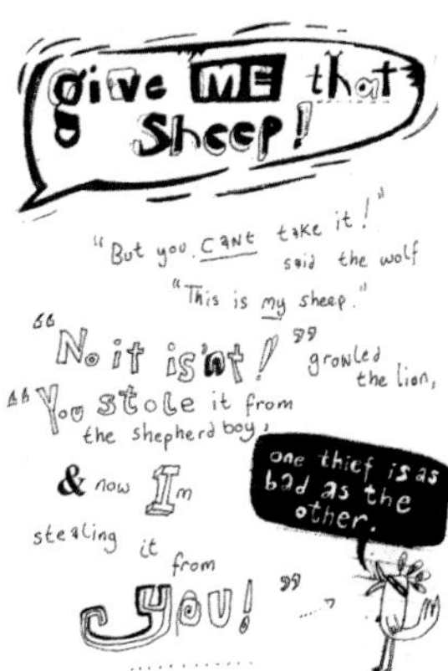

ANDY DAVIES : andyroberdavies@yahoo.com

Instructor Andrew Selby, Loughborough University, Leicestershire, United Kingdom

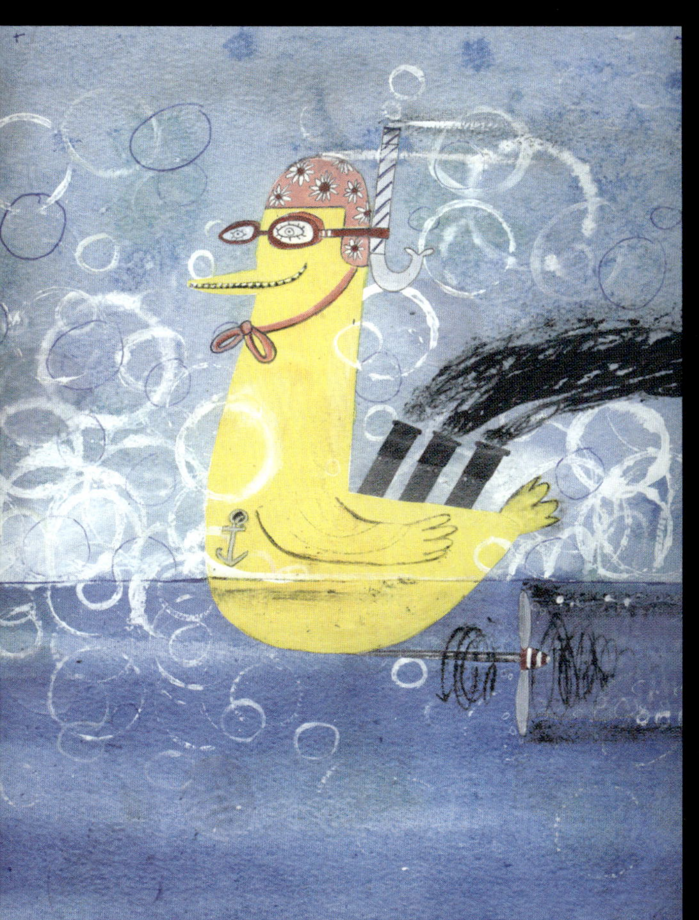

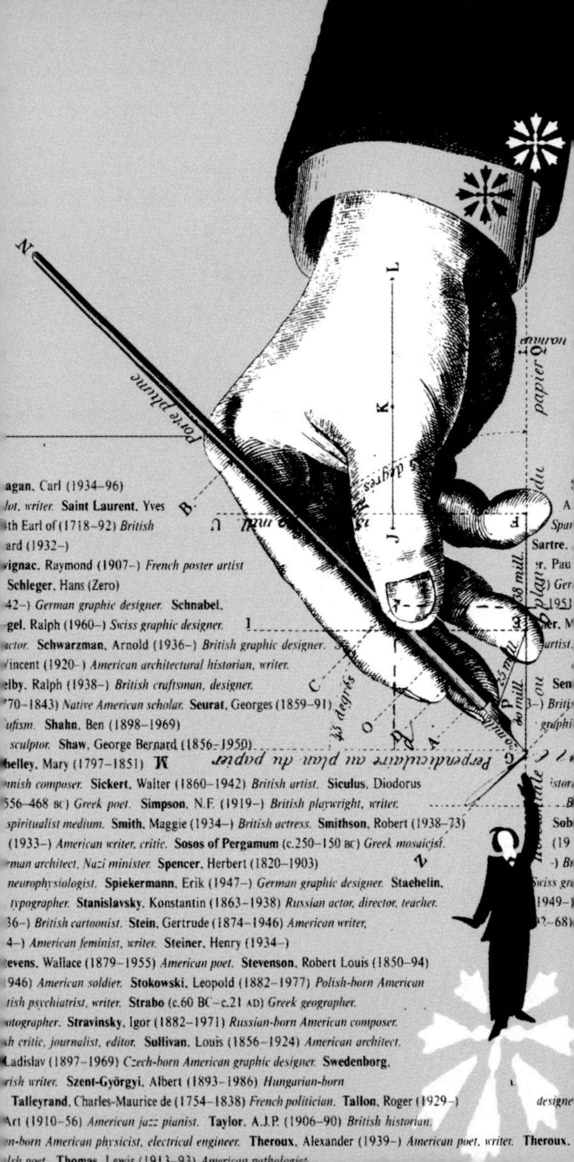

agan, Carl (1934–96)
lot, writer. **Saint Laurent**, Yves
th Earl of (1718–92) British
ard (1932–)
vignac, Raymond (1907–) French poster artist
Schleger, Hans (Zero)
42–) German graphic designer. **Schnabel**,
gel, Ralph (1960–) Swiss graphic designer.
ctor. **Schwarzman**, Arnold (1936–) British graphic designer.
Vincent (1920–) American architectural historian, writer.
elby, Ralph (1938–) British craftsman, designer.
70–1843) Native American scholar. **Seurat**, Georges (1859–91)
ufism. **Shahn**, Ben (1898–1969)
sculptor. **Shaw**, George Bernard (1856–1950)
helley, Mary (1797–1851)
nnish composer. **Sickert**, Walter (1860–1942) British artist. **Siculus**, Diodorus
556–468 BC) Greek poet. **Simpson**, N.F. (1919–) British playwright, writer.
spiritualist medium. **Smith**, Maggie (1934–) British actress. **Smithson**, Robert (1938–73)
(1933–) American writer, critic. **Sosos of Pergamum** (c.250–150 BC) Greek mosaicist.
rman architect, Nazi minister. **Spencer**, Herbert (1820–1903)
neurophysiologist. **Spiekermann**, Erik (1947–) German graphic designer. **Staehelin**,
typographer. **Stanislavsky**, Konstantin (1863–1938) Russian actor, director, teacher.
36–) British cartoonist. **Stein**, Gertrude (1874–1946) American writer,
4–) American feminist, writer. **Steiner**, Henry (1934–)
tevens, Wallace (1879–1955) American poet. **Stevenson**, Robert Louis (1850–94)
946) American soldier. **Stokowski**, Leopold (1882–1977) Polish-born American
tish psychiatrist, writer. **Strabo** (c.60 BC–c.21 AD) Greek geographer.
otographer. **Stravinsky**, Igor (1882–1971) Russian-born American composer.
sh critic, journalist, editor. **Sullivan**, Louis (1856–1924) American architect.
Ladislav (1897–1969) Czech-born American graphic designer. **Swedenborg**,
rish writer. **Szent-Györgyi**, Albert (1893–1986) Hungarian-born
Talleyrand, Charles-Maurice de (1754–1838) French politician. **Tallon**, Roger (1929–)
Art (1910–56) American jazz pianist. **Taylor**, A.J.P. (1906–90) British historian.
m-born American physicist, electrical engineer. **Theroux**, Alexander (1939–) American poet, writer. **Theroux**,
lsh poet. **Thomas**, Lewis (1913–93) American pathologist.

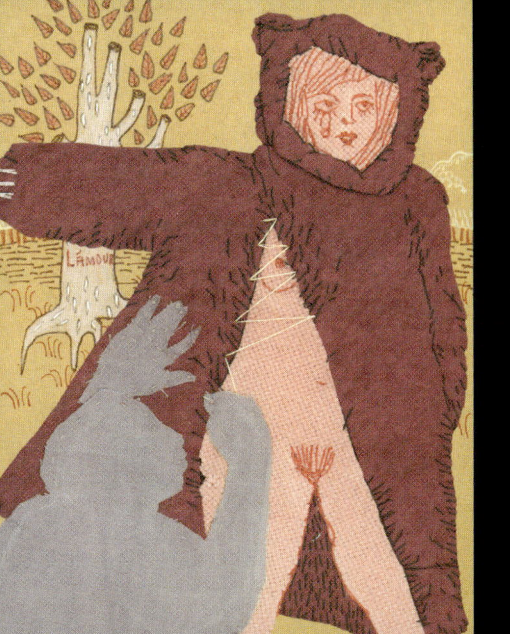
L'AMOUR

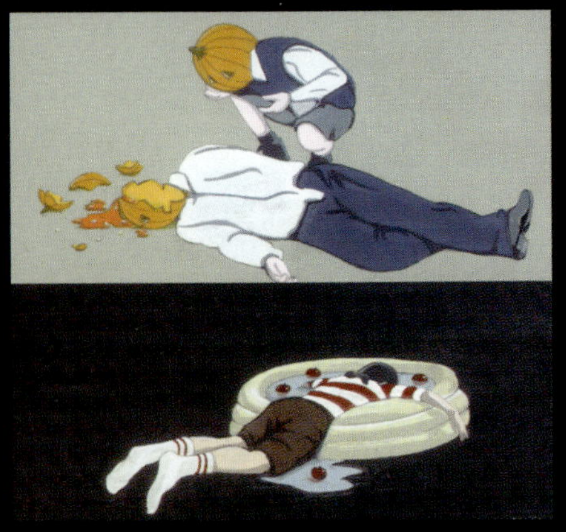

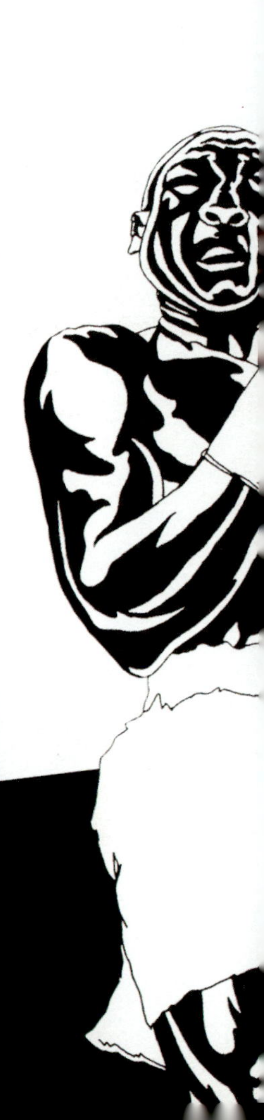

above: KIERSTEN ESSENPREIS
kiersten@youfail.com
Instructor Jordin Isip, Pratt Institute, New York

right: DANIEL GALVANAUGH
rockwell56@nyc.rr.com
*Instructor Marshall Arisman, School of Visual Arts,
New York*

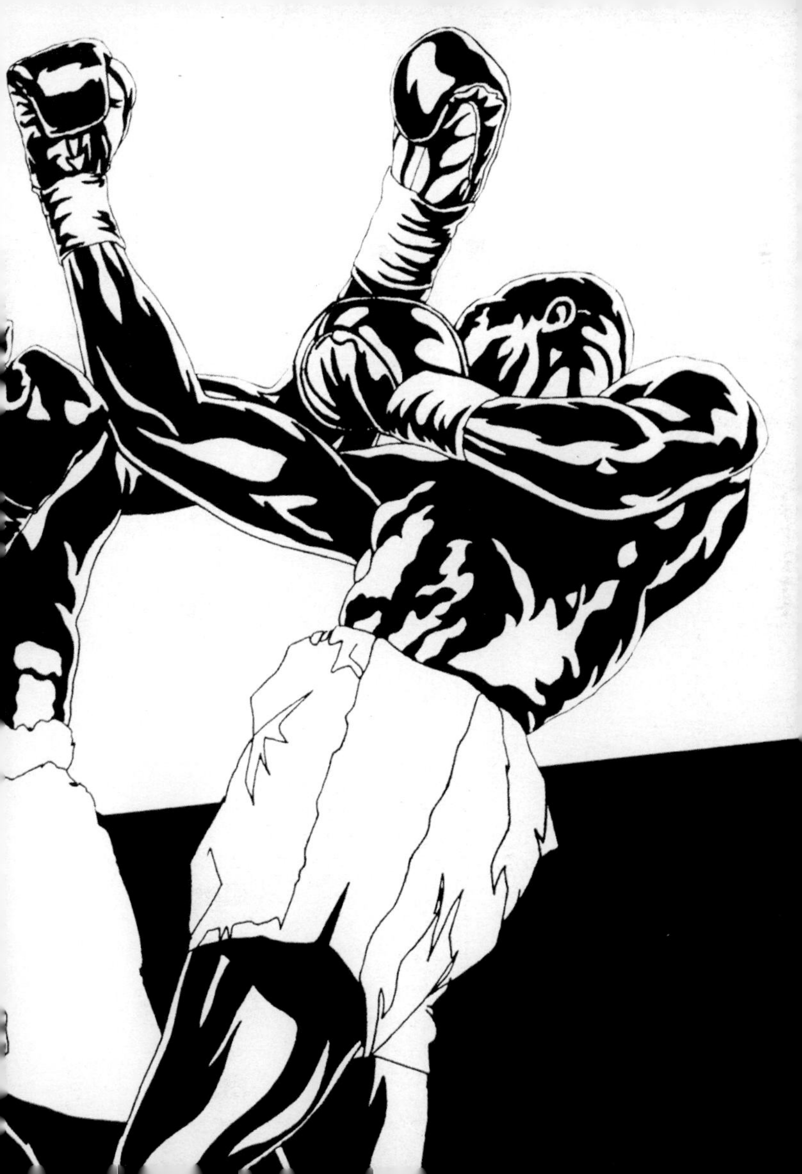

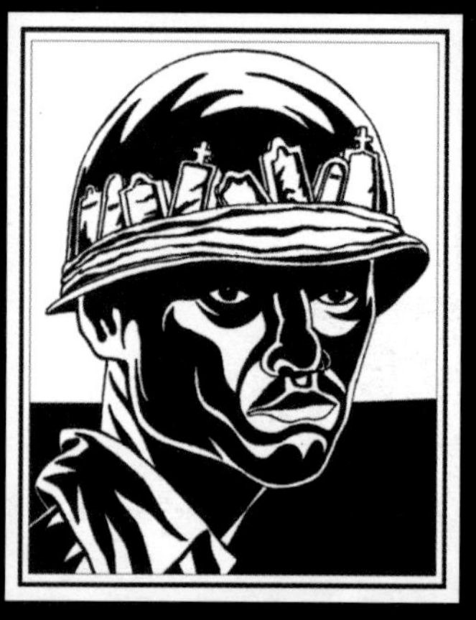

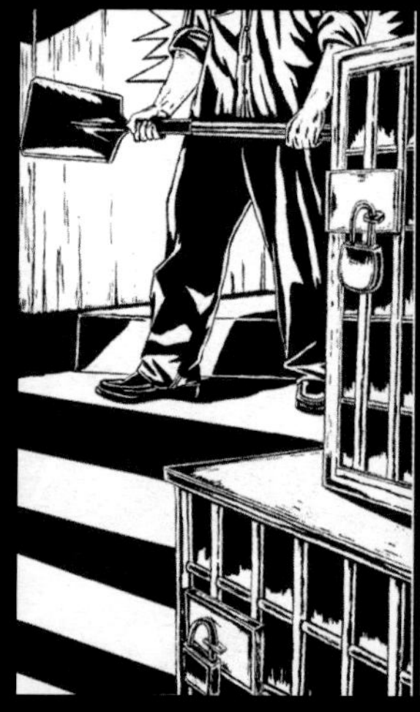

above: DANIEL GALVANAUGH : rockwell56@nyc.rr.com
Instructor Marshall Arisman, School of Visual Arts, New York

right: GARY GARAY : gary.garay@verizon.net
Instructor Aaron Smith, Art Center, California

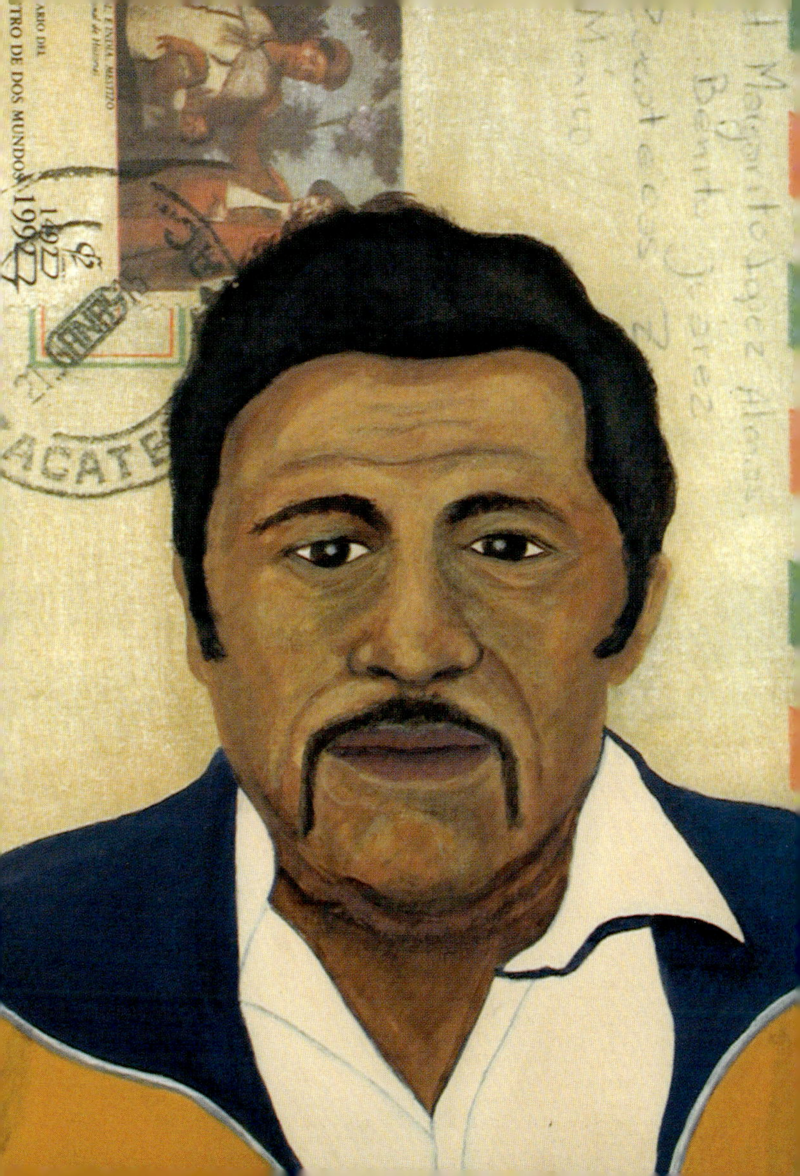
Margarita Sáez Alcalá
Benito Juárez
Zacatecas
México
1 Mayo 1992
ACATE

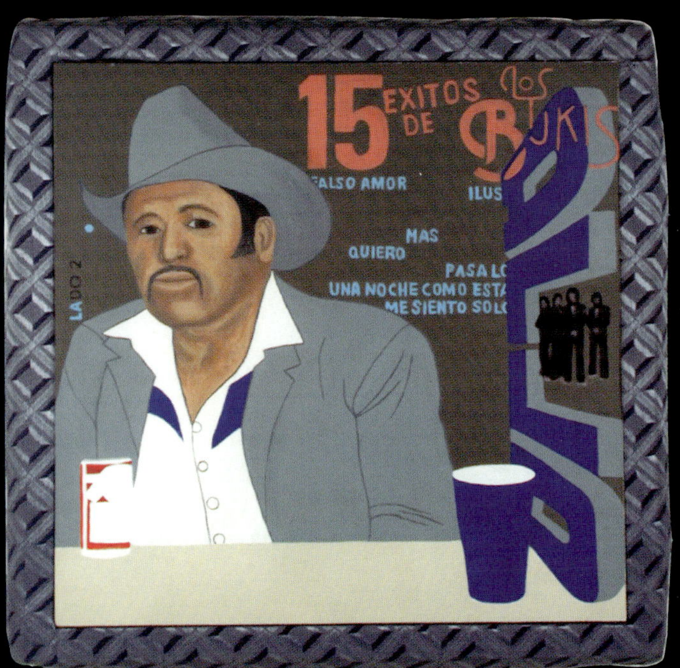

GARY GARAY : gary.garay@verizon.net
Instructor Aaron Smith, Art Center, California

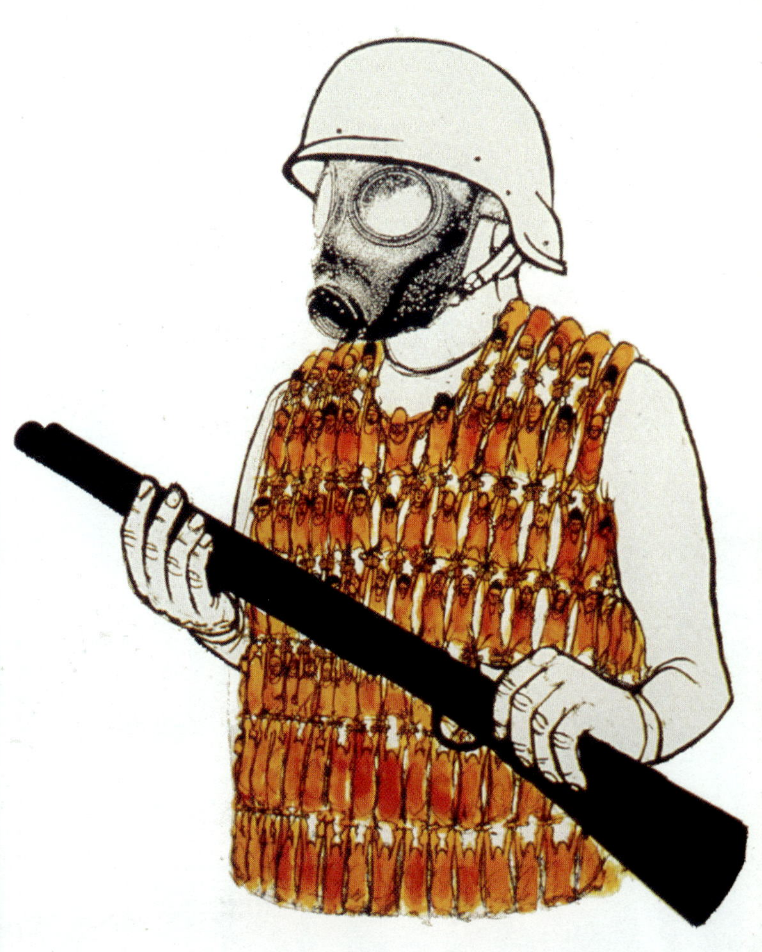

JASON GREENBERG : hornsbynation@hotmail.com
Instructor Tom Garrett, Minneapolis College of Art & Design, Minnesota

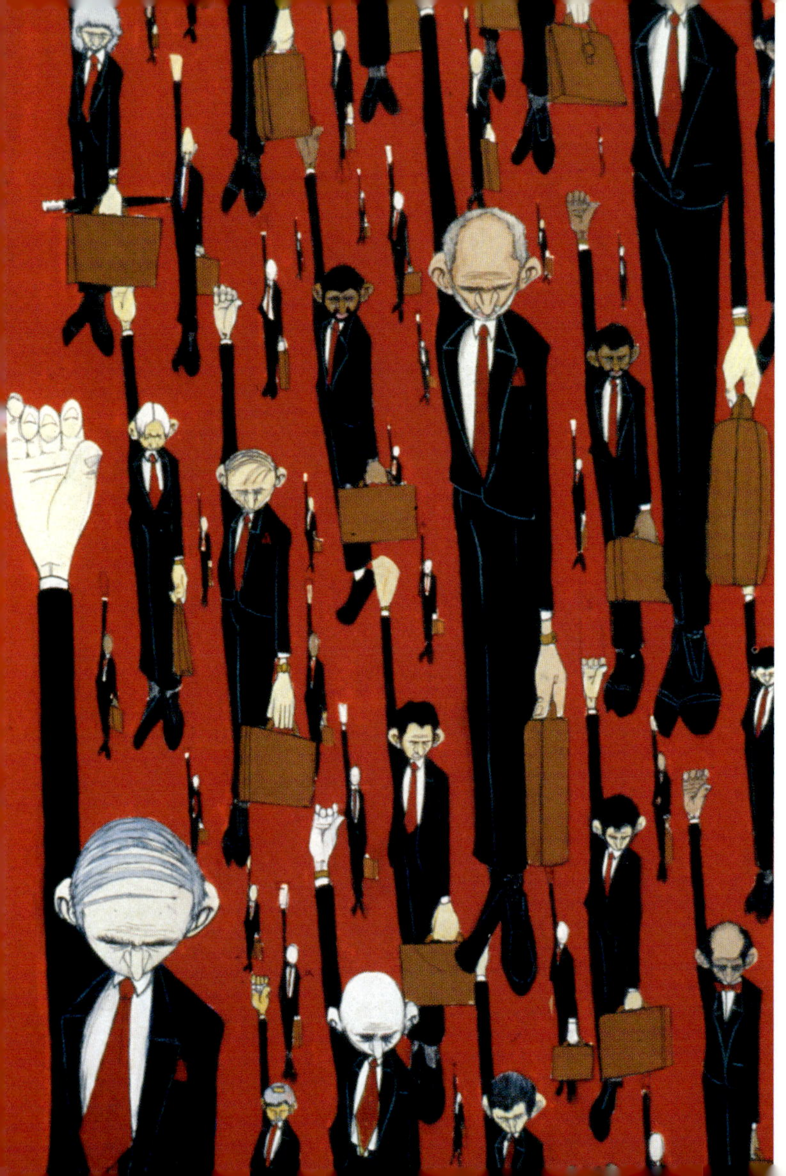

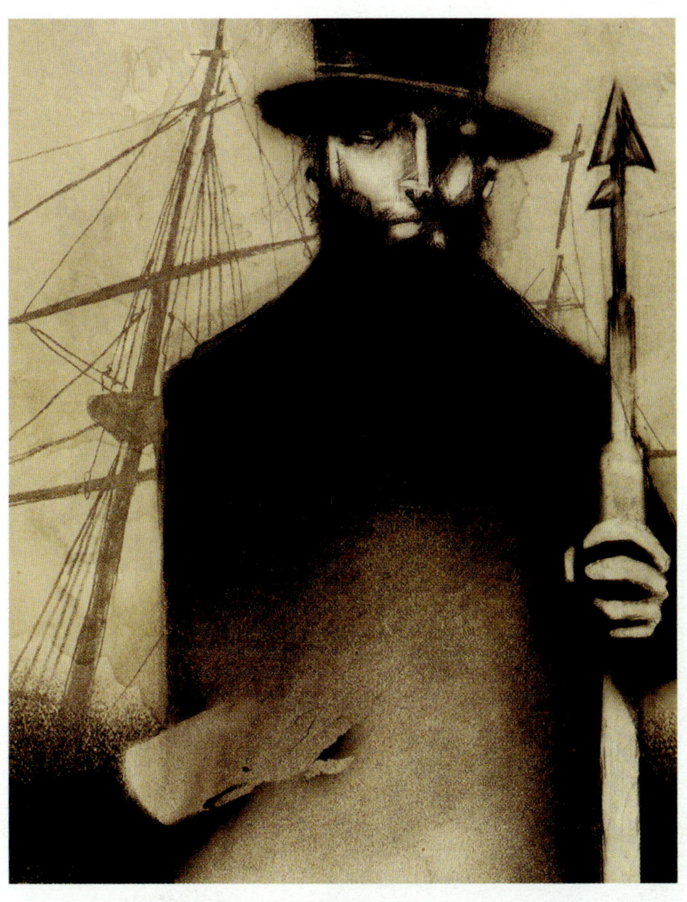

left: JASON GREENBERG : hornsbynation@hotmail.com
Instructor Tom Garrett, Minneapolis College of Art & Design, Minnesota

above: CHRIS HAJNY : teenwolfdude@aol.com
Instructor Tom Garrett, Minneapolis College of Art & Design, Minnesota

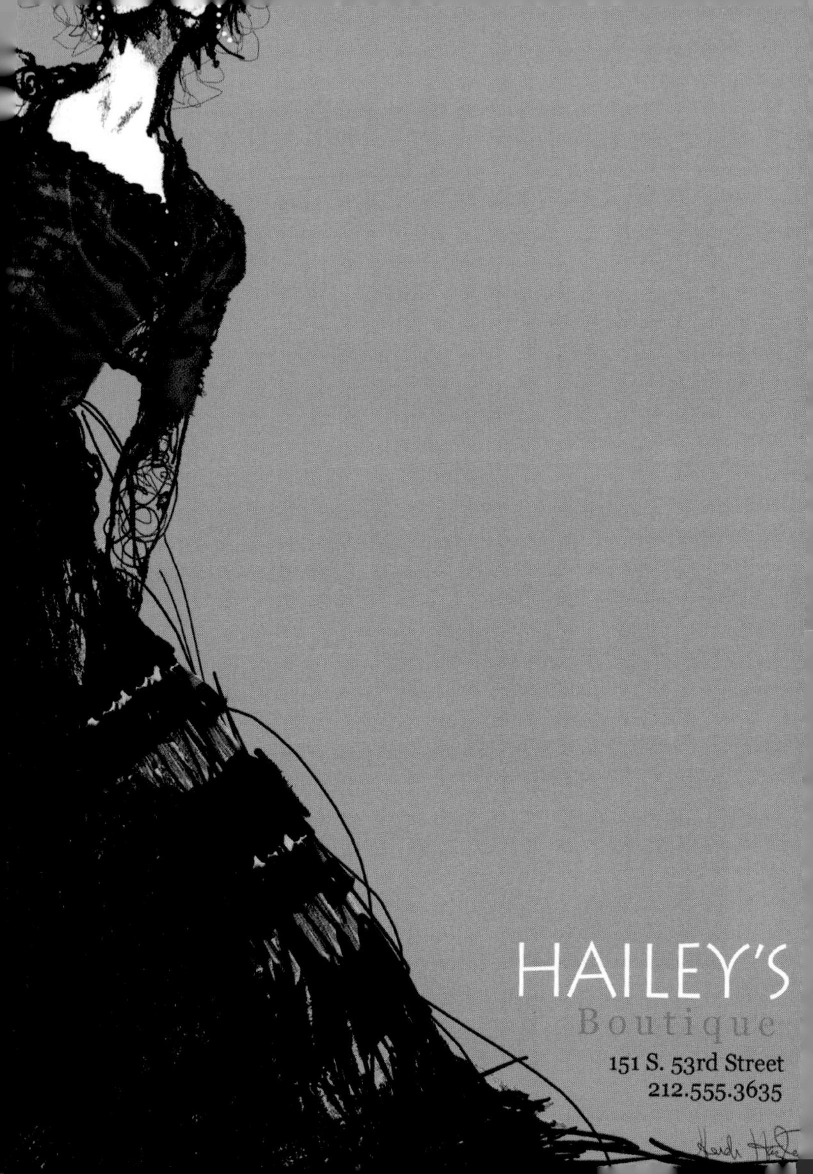
HAILEY'S
Boutique
151 S. 53rd Street
212.555.3635

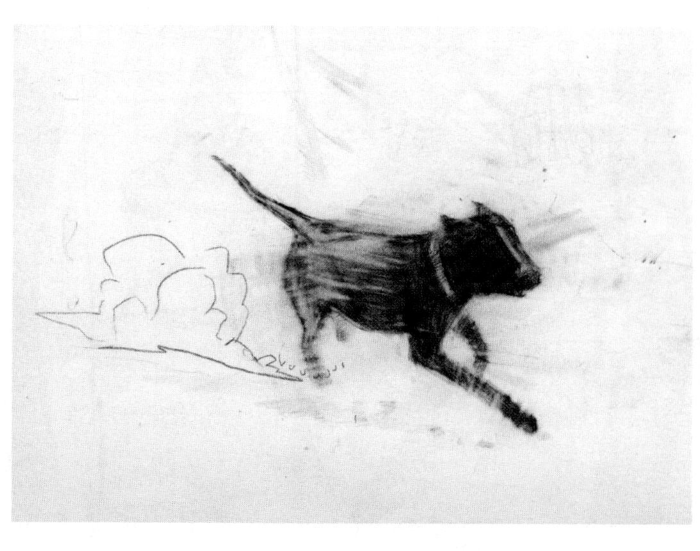

left: HEIDI HAZLEY : lov4art1@aol.com
Instructor Megan Berkenheiser, University of the Arts, Pennsylvania

above: CHRIS HAJNY : teenwolfdude@aol.com
Instructor Tom Garrett, Minneapolis College of Art & Design, Minnesota

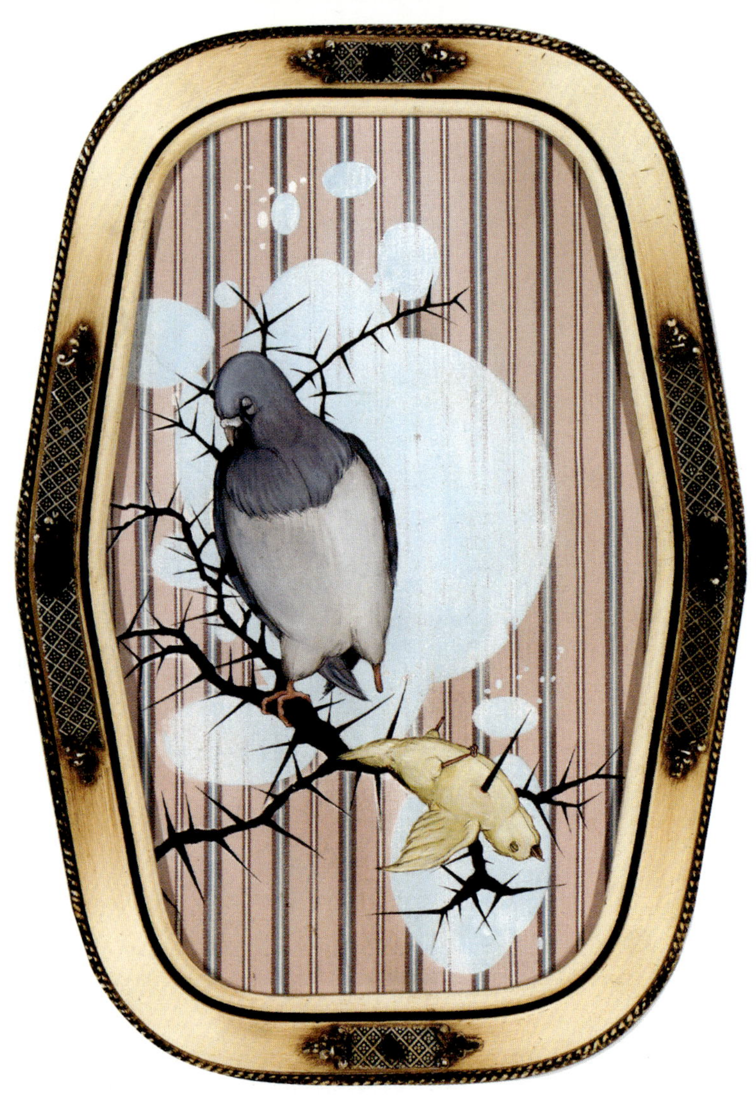

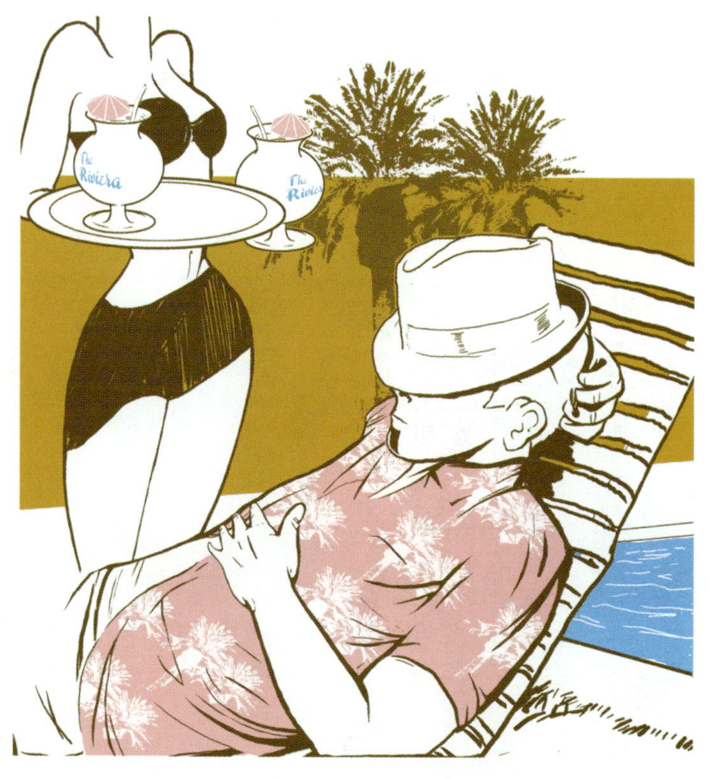

left: PAMELA HENDERSON : pamela@pamelahenderson.com
Art Center, California

above: JAMES J. HOLZMAN : james@holzmanillustration.com
Instructor Rebecca Bradley, The Art Institute of Boston, Massachusetts

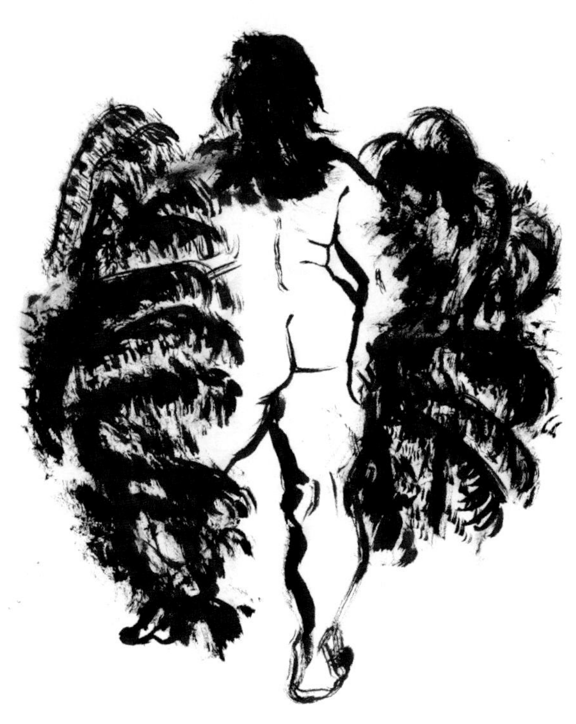

above: PAUL HOPPE : paulhoppe@web.de
Instructor Carol Fabricatore, School of Visual Arts, New York

right: STEVEN E. HUGHES : sehughe1@kent.edu
Instructor Jerry Kalback, Kent State University, Ohio

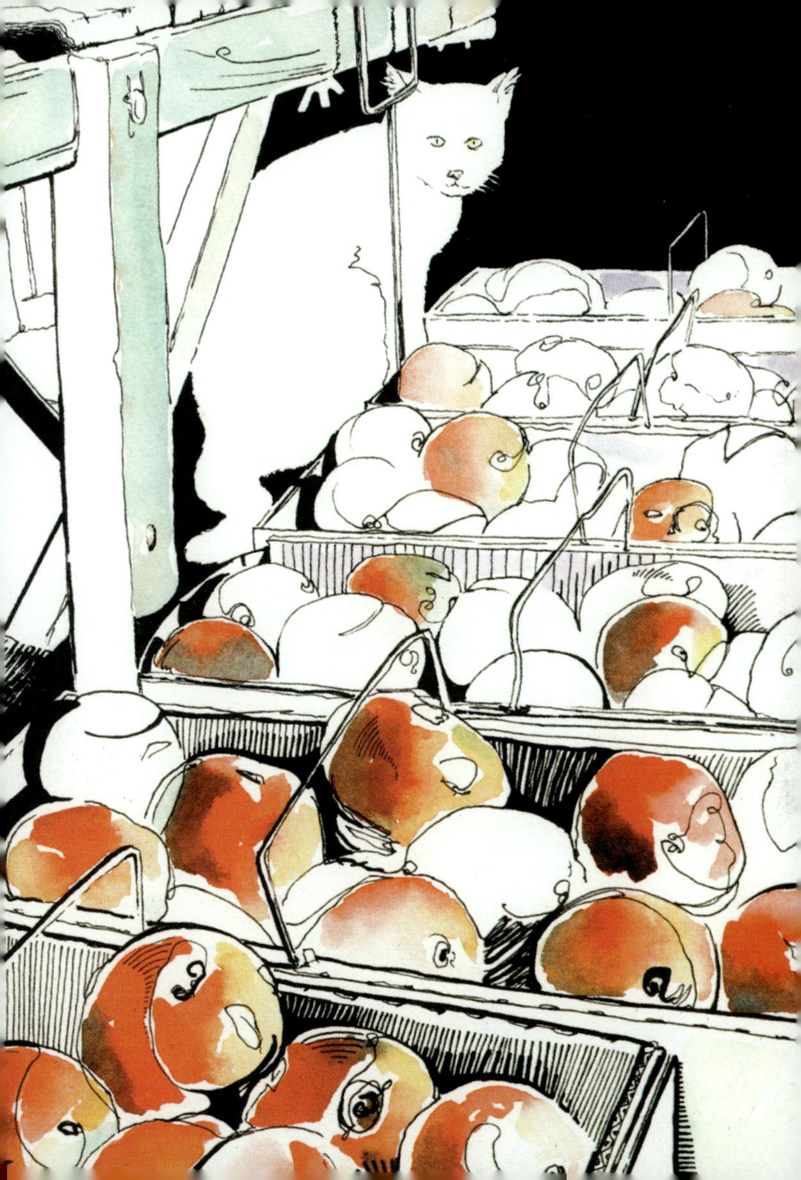

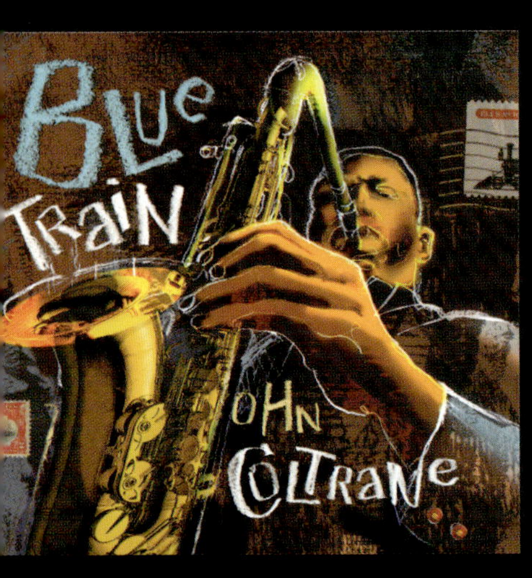

STEVEN E. HUGHES : sehughe1@kent.edu

Instructor Jerry Kalback, Kent State University, Ohio

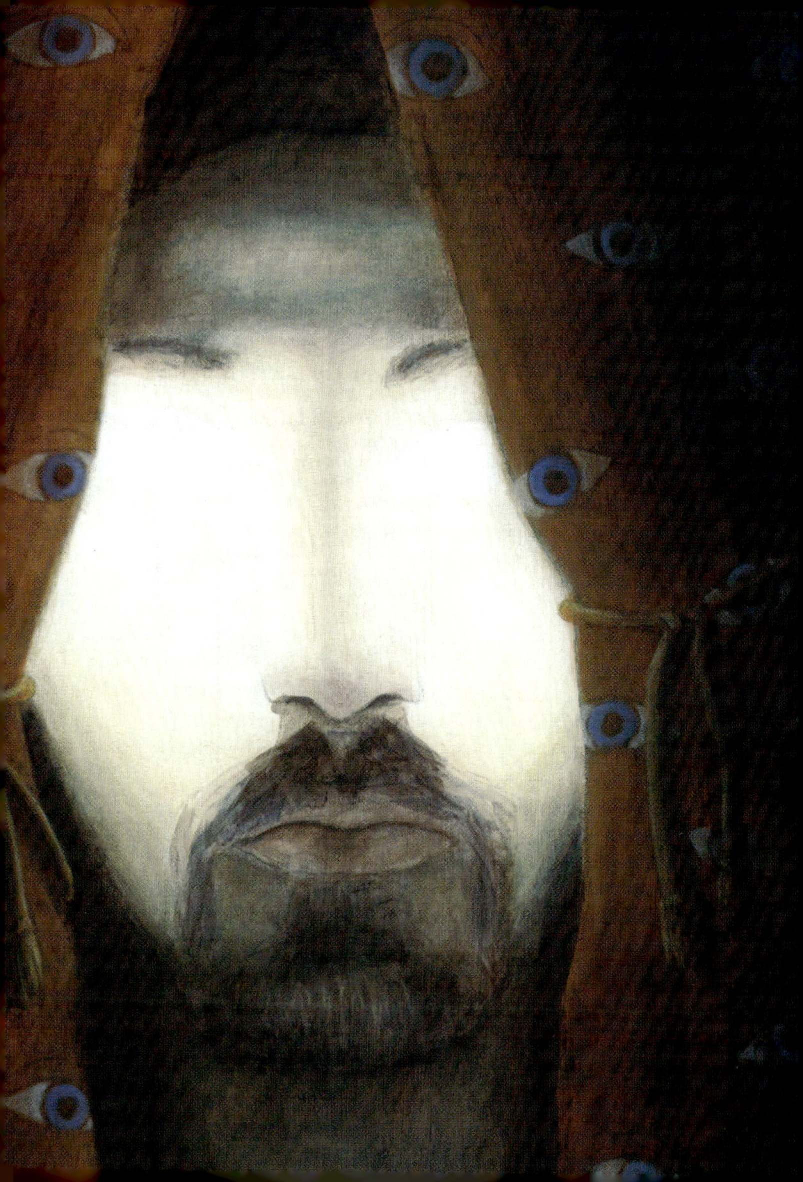

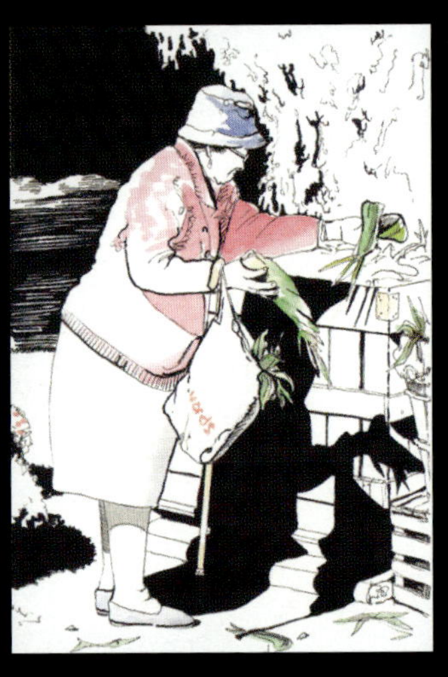
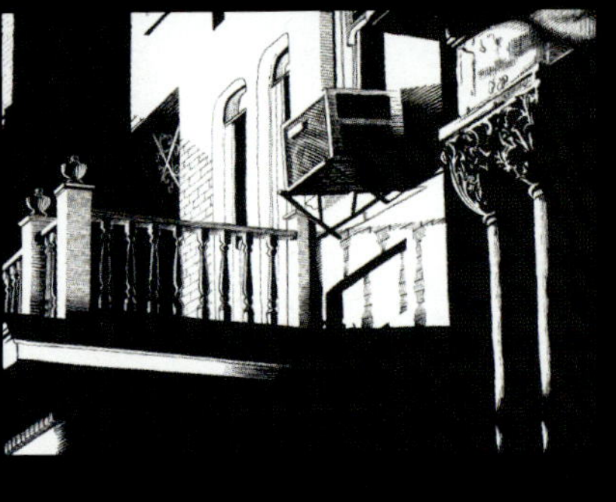

STEVEN E. HUGHES : sehughe1@kent.edu
Instructor Jerry Kalback, Kent State University, Ohio

The Peaceable Kingdom

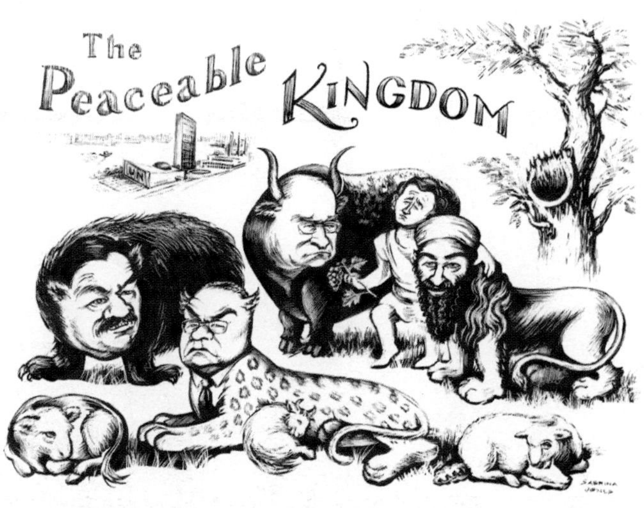

SABRINA JONES : sabjonze@yahoo.com
Instructor David Sandlin, Pratt Institute, New York

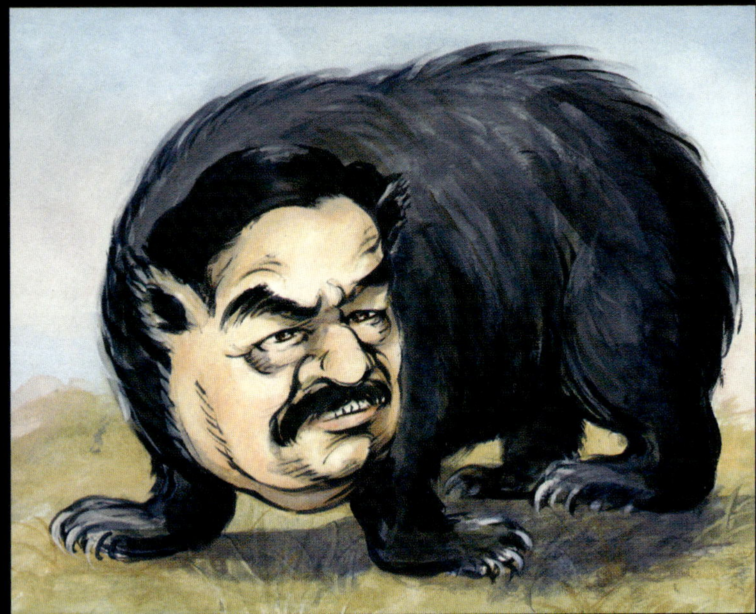

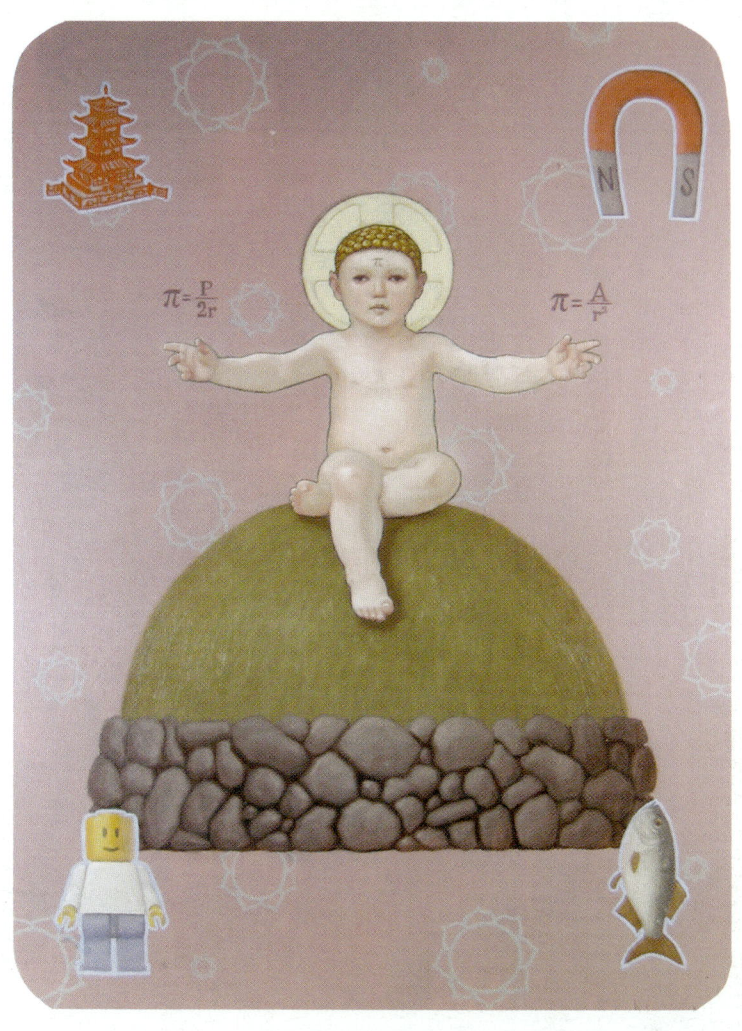

YOUNG SUK KIM : youngkim2483@yahoo.com
Instructor Aaron Smith, Art Center, California

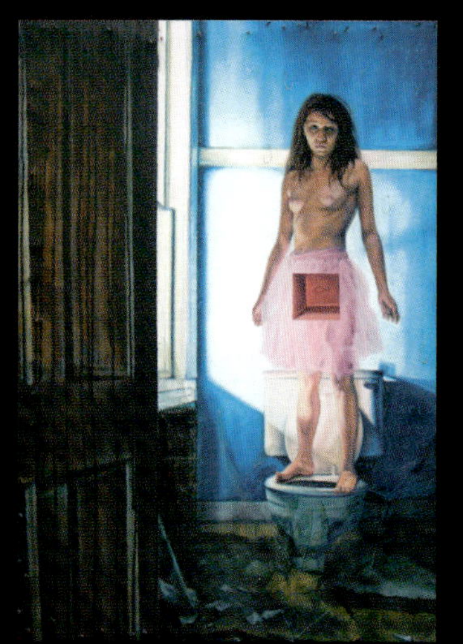
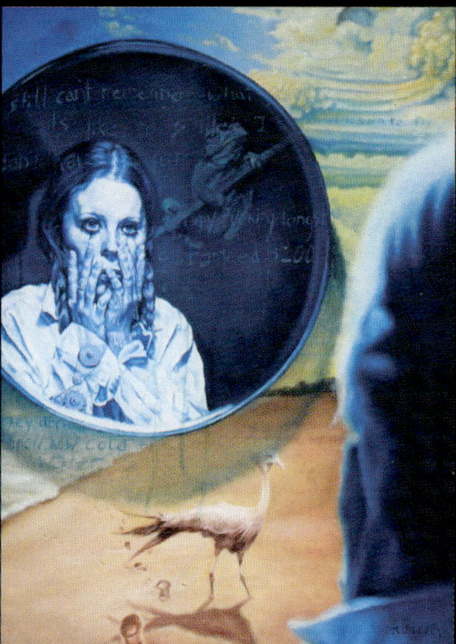
still can't remember what

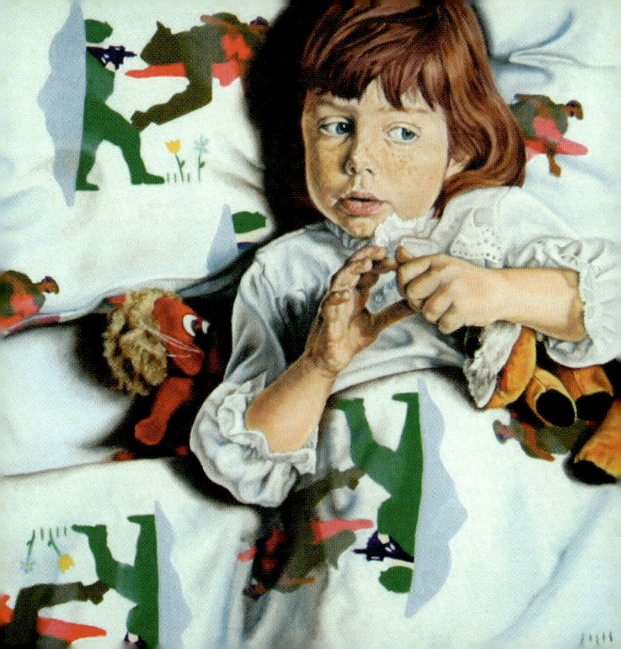

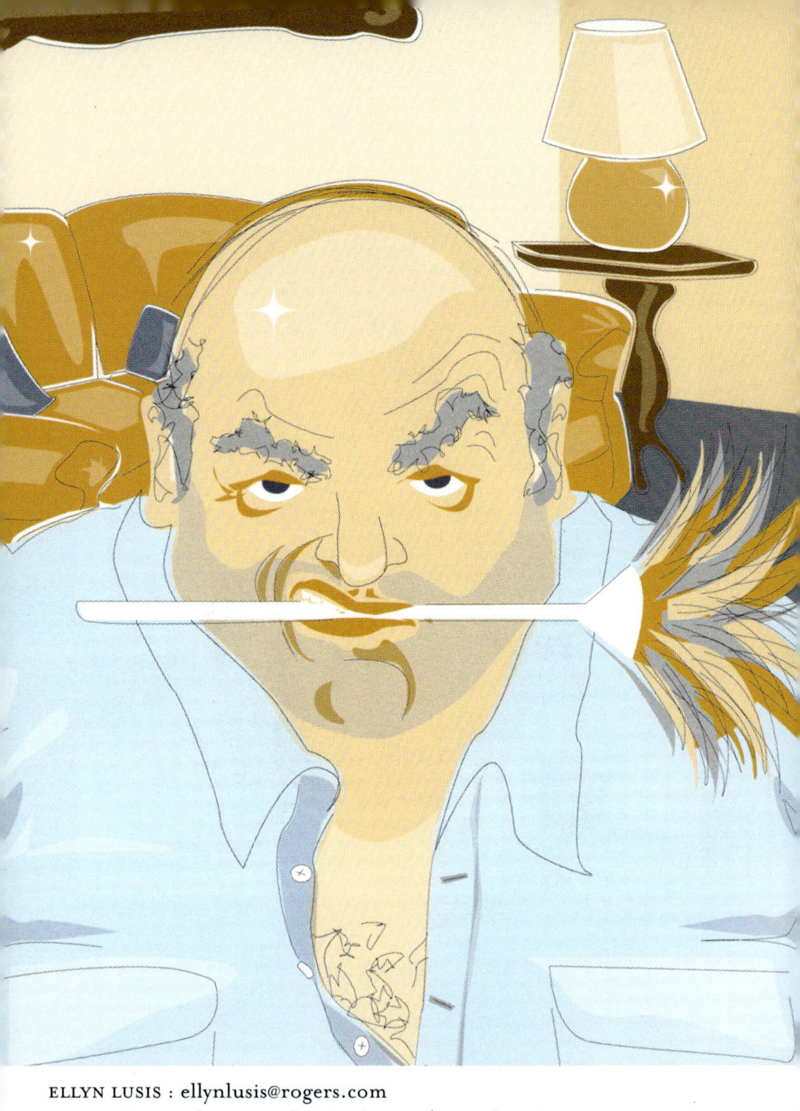

ELLYN LUSIS : ellynlusis@rogers.com
Instructor Riccardo Stampatori, Sheridan College, Toronto, Canada

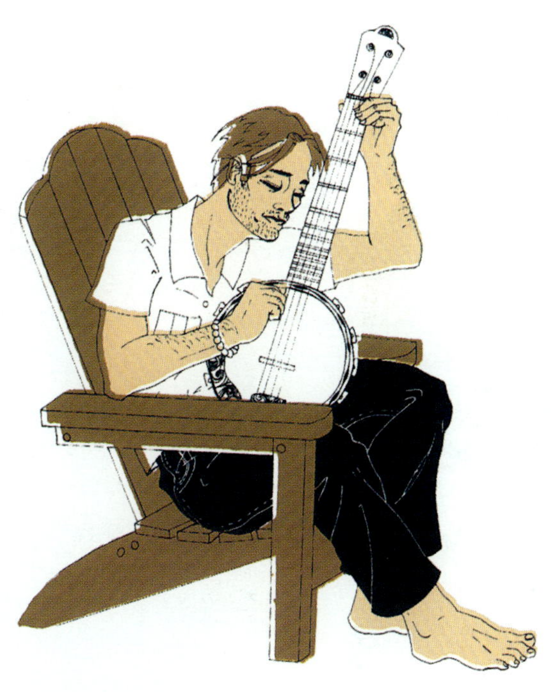

JULIA MINAMATA : jm@juliaminamata.com
Instructor Gary Taxali, Sheridan College, Toronto, Canada

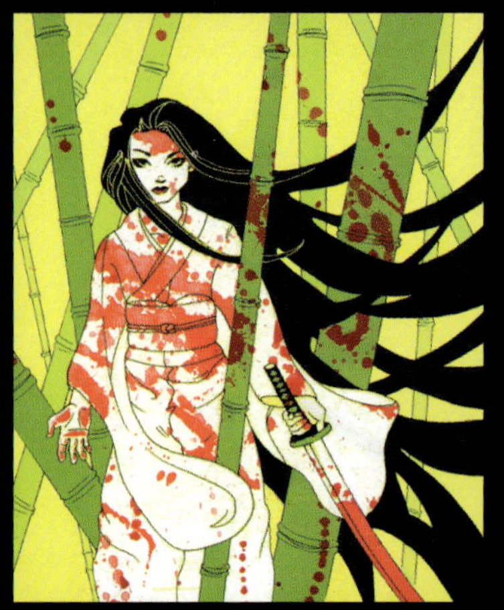

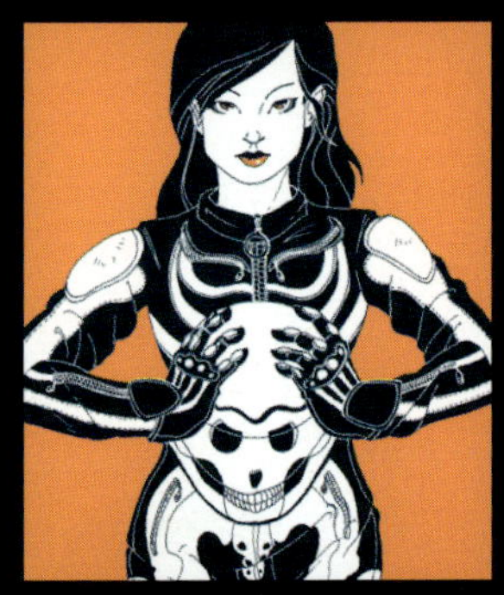

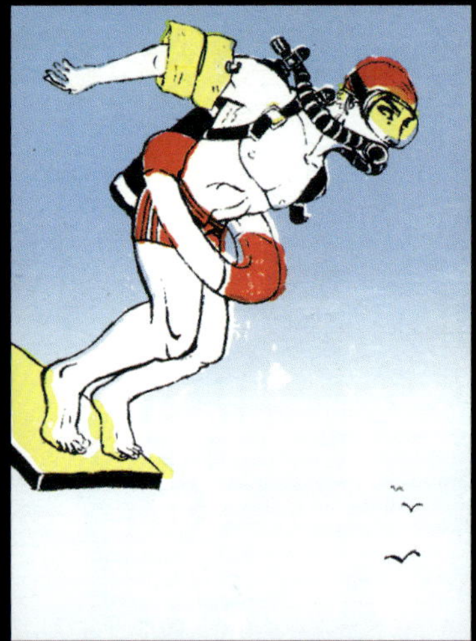

JULIA MINAMATA : jm@juliaminamata.com
Instructor Gary Taxali, Sheridan College, Toronto, Canada

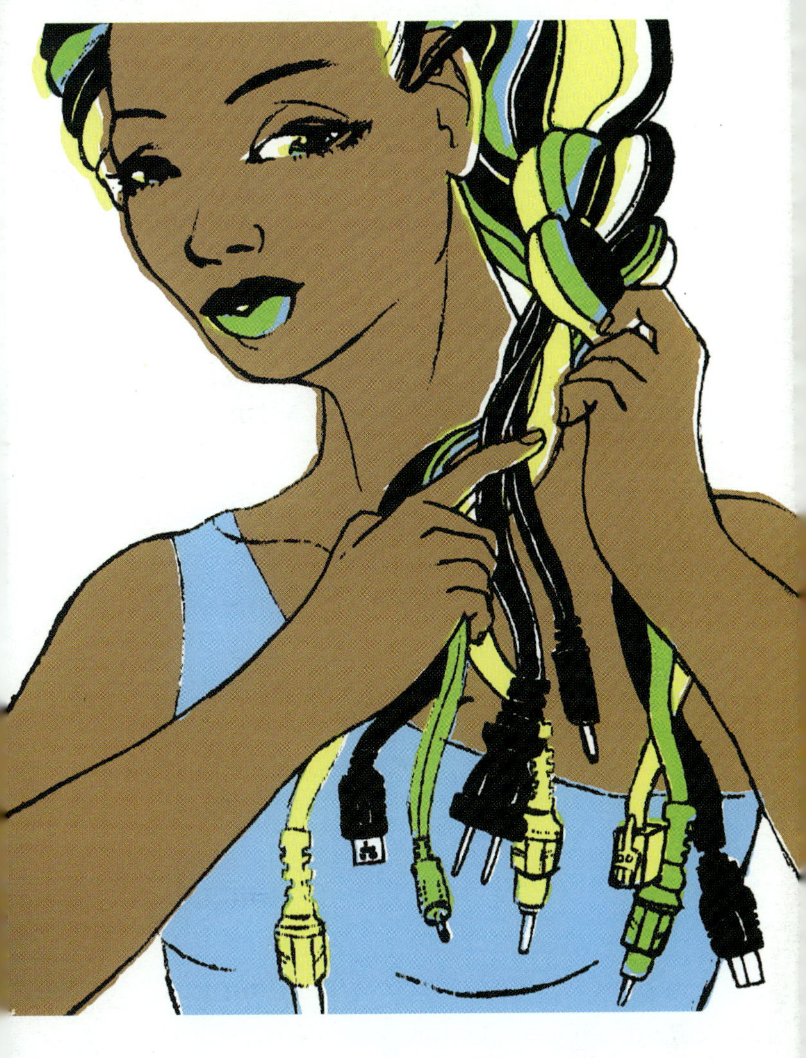

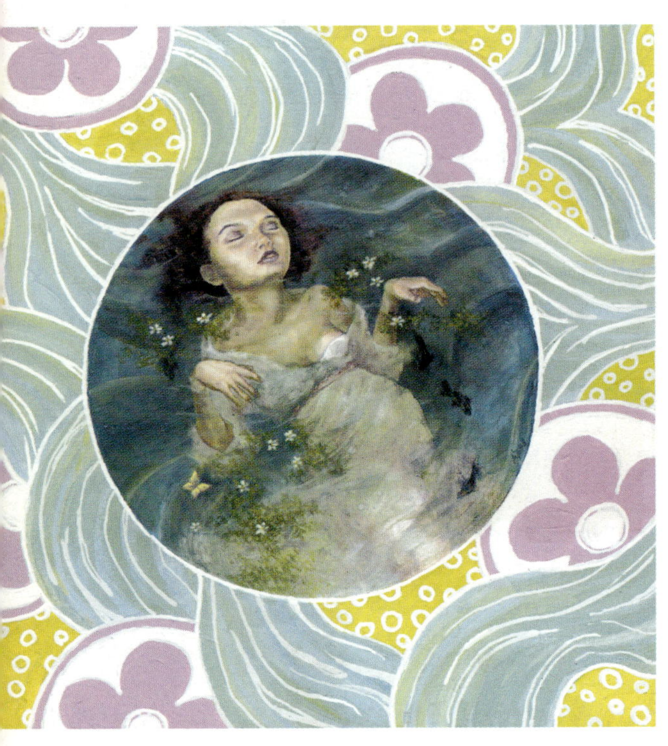

ANDREA LYNN PETERSON : artistALP@yahoo.com
Instructor Joan Mansfield, East Carolina University, North Carolina

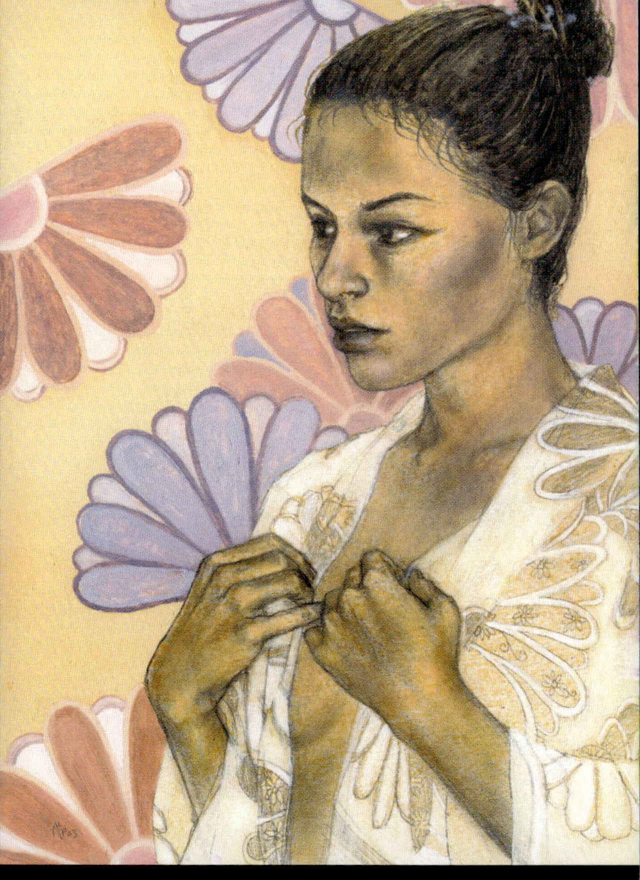

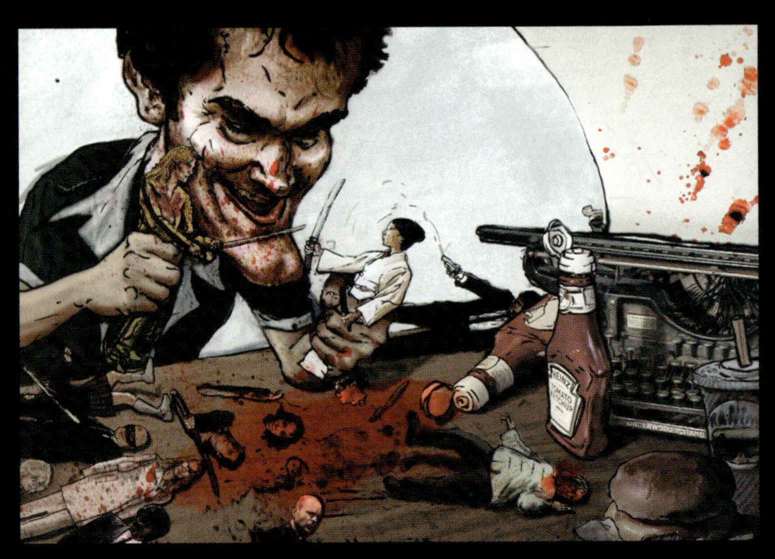

above: RAUL RODRIGUEZ : raulrallen@yahoo.com
Instructor Rob Zammarchi, The Art Institute of Boston, Massachusetts

right: ERIC SEAT : eric@ericseat.com
Instructor Sterling Hundley, Virginia Commonwealth University, Virginia

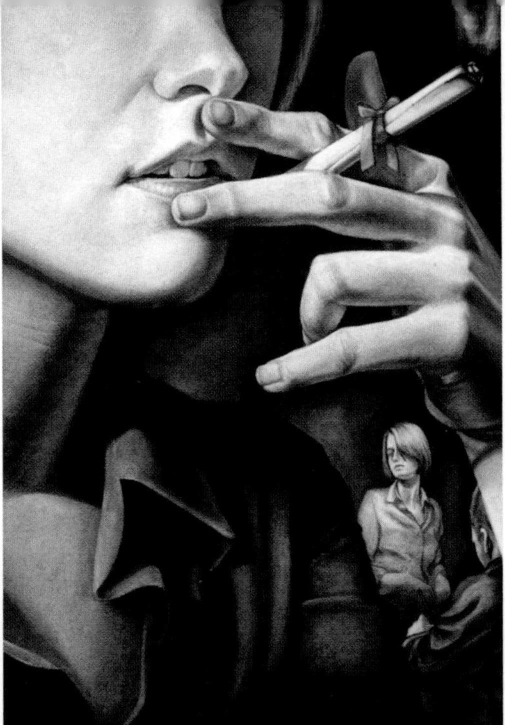

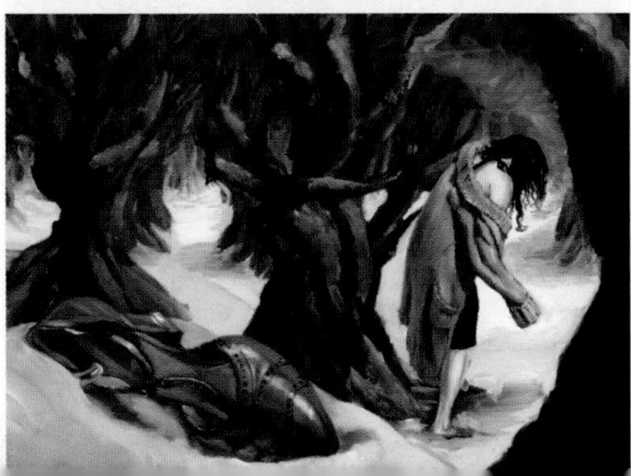

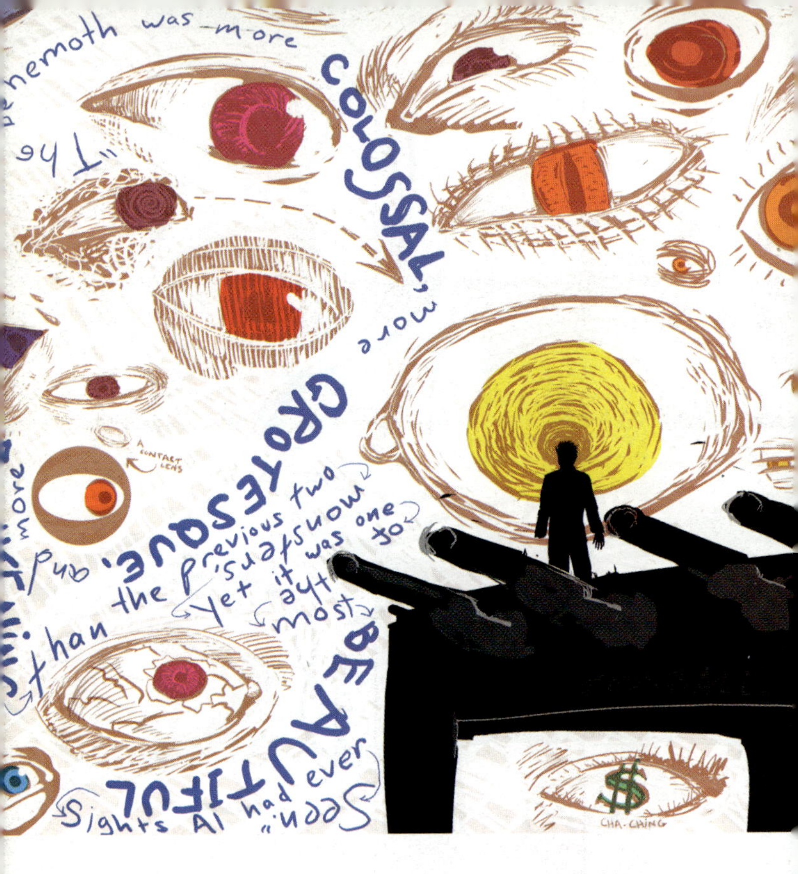

ERIC SEAT : eric@ericseat.com
Instructor Sterling Hundley, Virginia Commonwealth University, Virginia

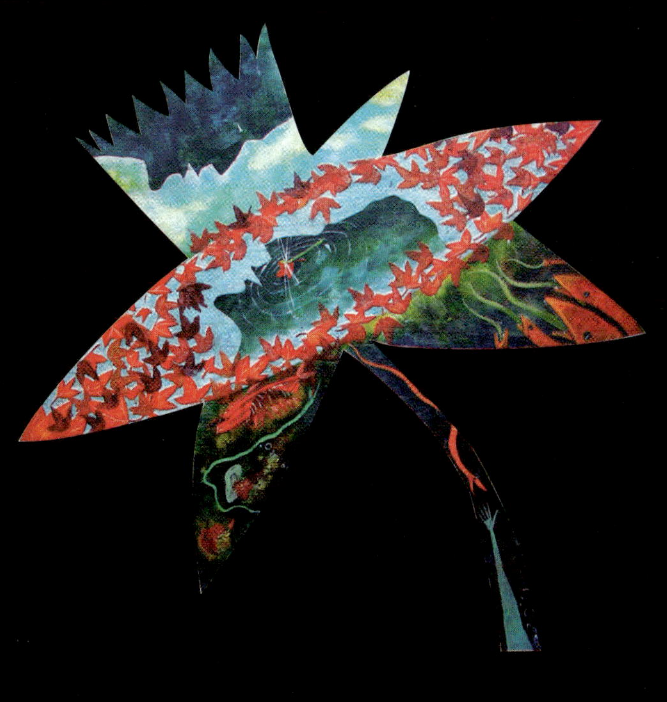

PAUL SMITH : paulsmithillustrator@yahoo.co.uk
Instructor Andrew Selby, Loughborough University, Leicestershire, United Kingdom

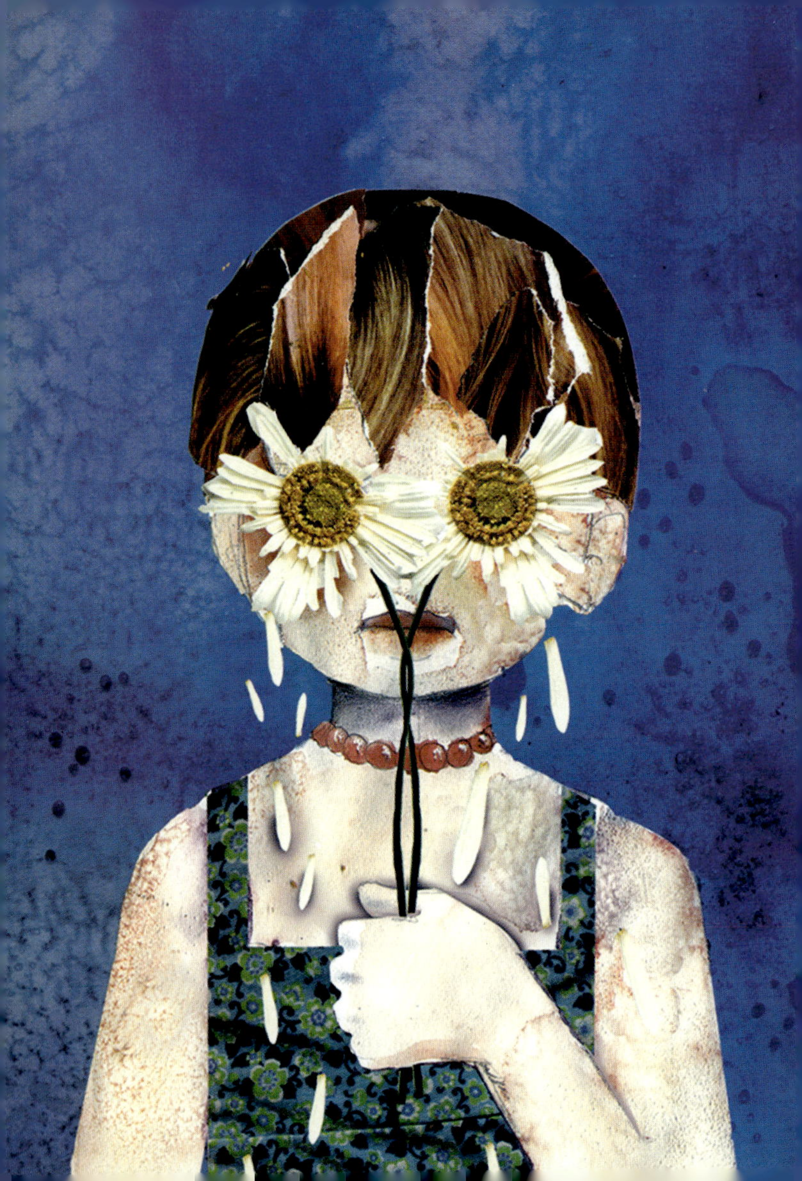

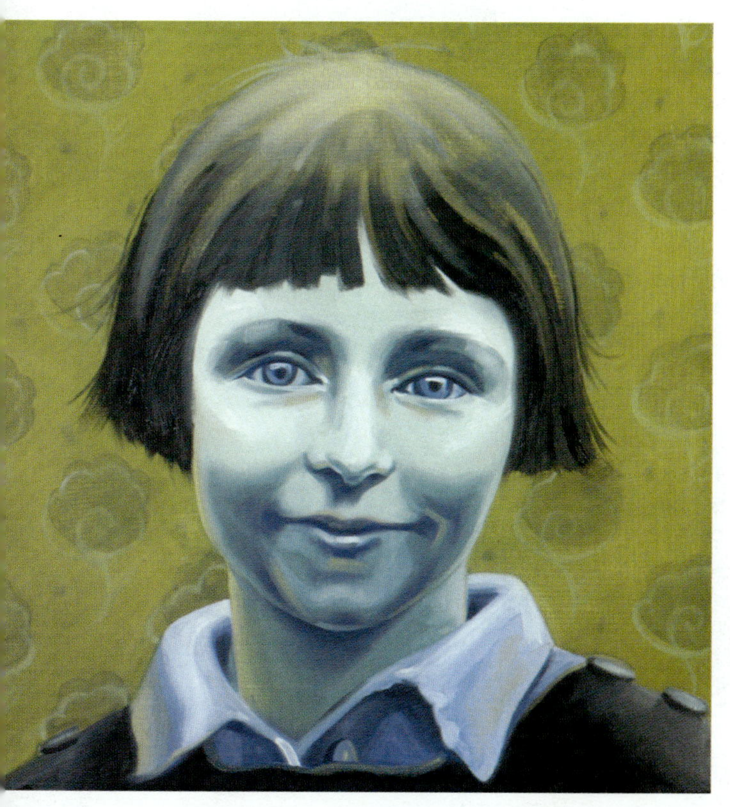

left: CHRIS SNEE : stickfiguresnee@aol.com
Instructor Jon Krause, The Tyler School of Art, Pennsylvania

above: MARIAN STEWART : marian.stewart@cox.net
Instructor George Zebot, California State University, Long Beach

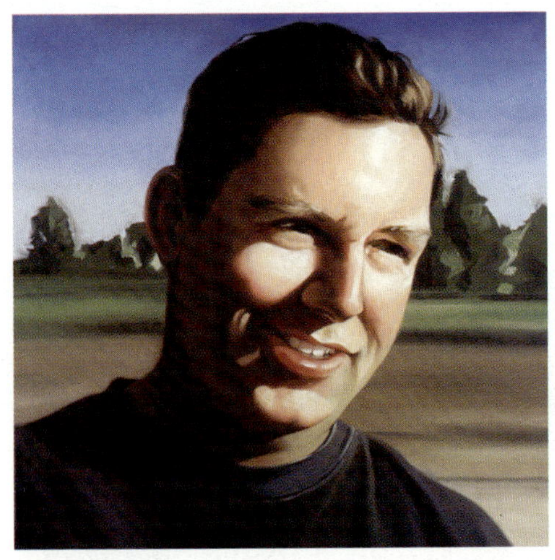

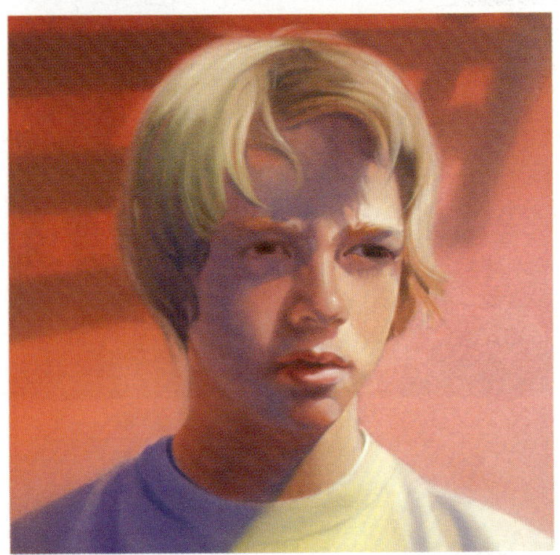

MARIAN STEWART : marian.stewart@cox.net
Instructor George Zebot, California State University, Long Beach

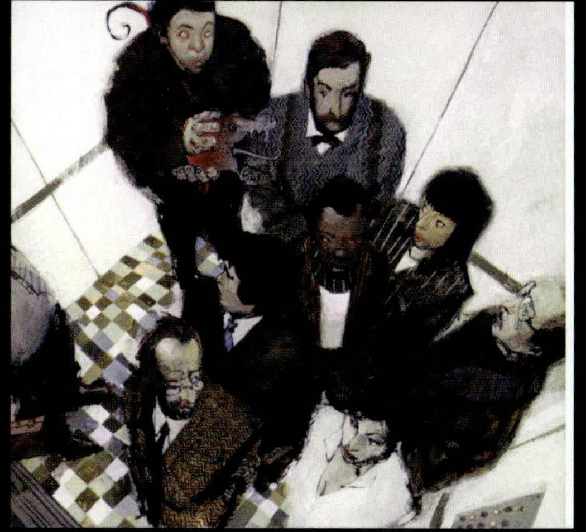

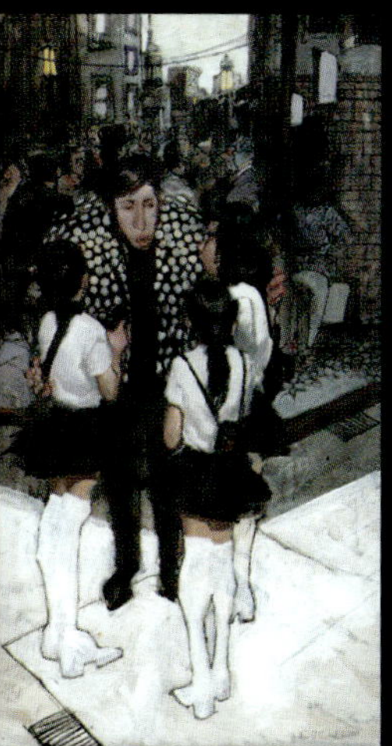

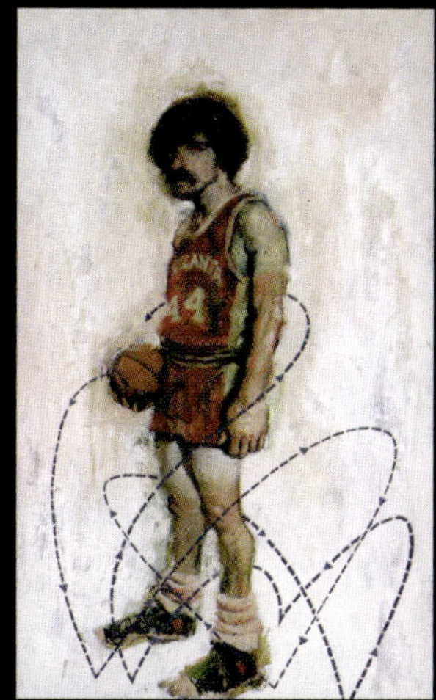

FRANK STOCKTON : stockton@artcenter.edu

Instructor Aaron Smith, Art Center, California

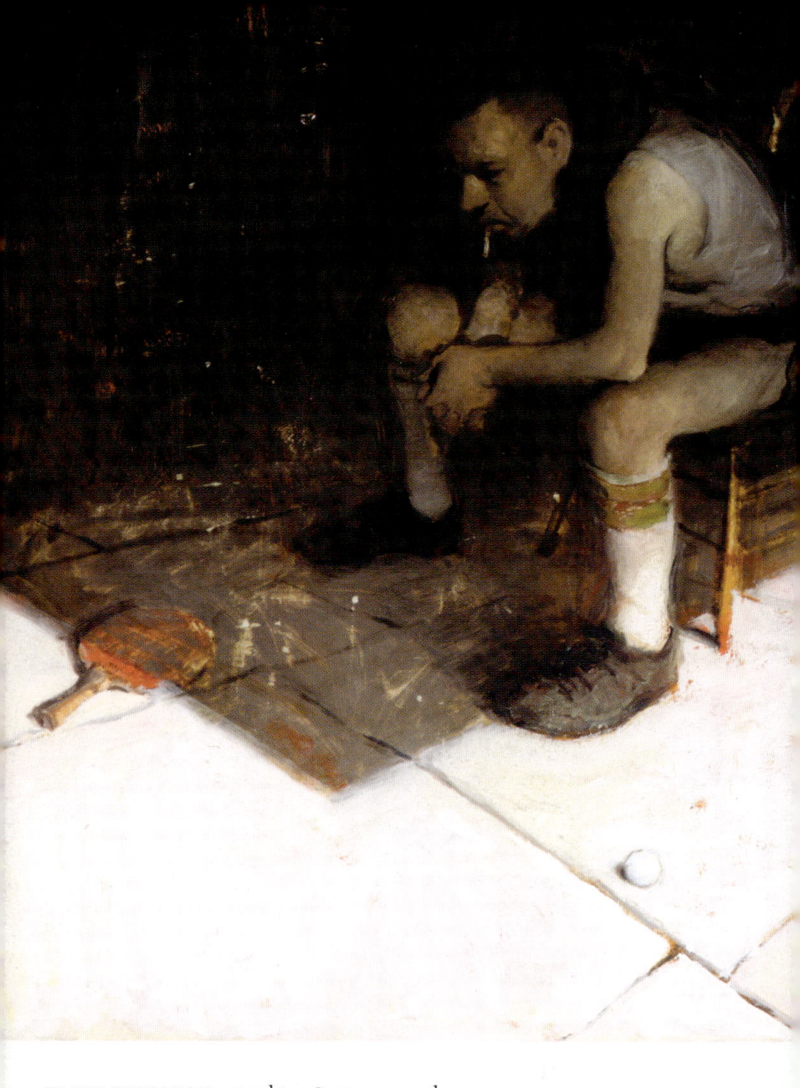

FRANK STOCKTON : stockton@artcenter.edu
Instructor Aaron Smith, Art Center, California

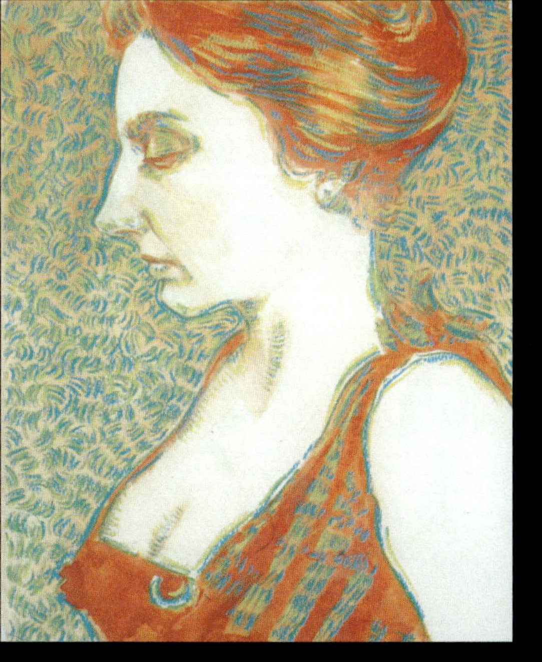

FALON STUTZMAN : falon3994@yahoo.com

Instructor Ron Skidmore, Garrett College, Maryland

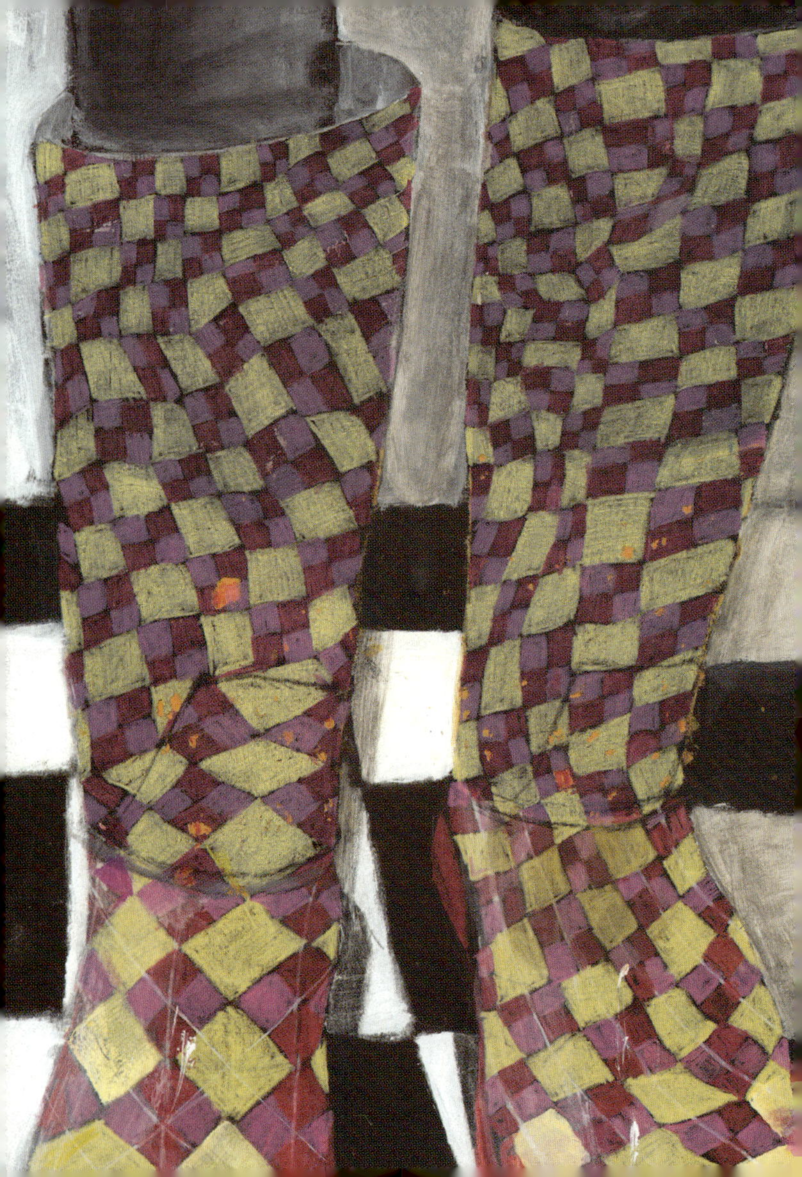

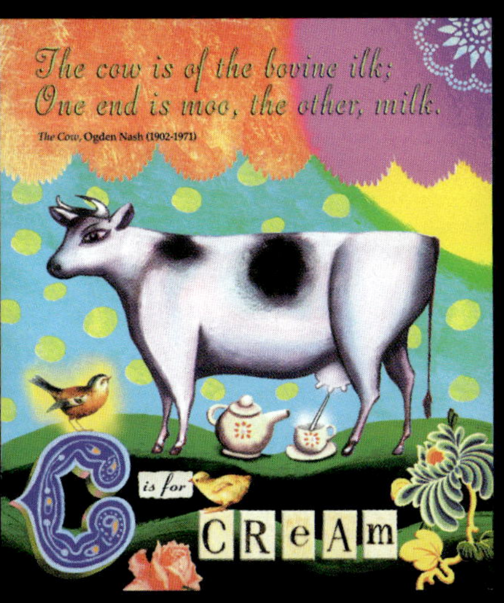

The cow is of the bovine ilk;
One end is moo, the other, milk.
The Cow, Ogden Nash (1902-1971)
C is for
CReAm

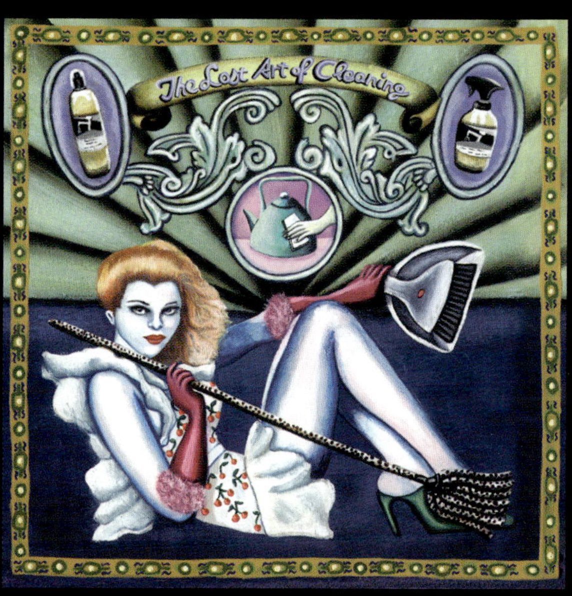

SHARON TANCREDI : s.tancredi@btintement.com

Instructor Geoff Grandfield, Middlesex University, London

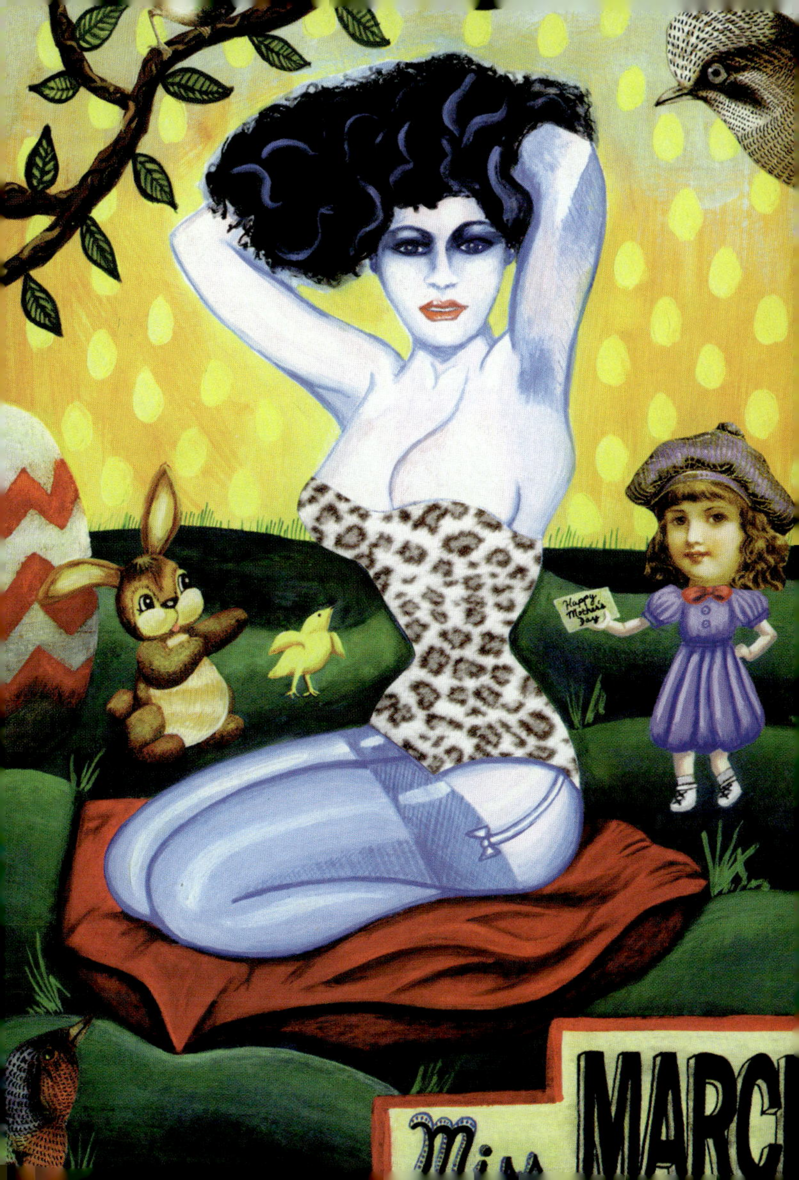

Happy Mother's Day
Miss MARCH

The WOLf and 7 Kids

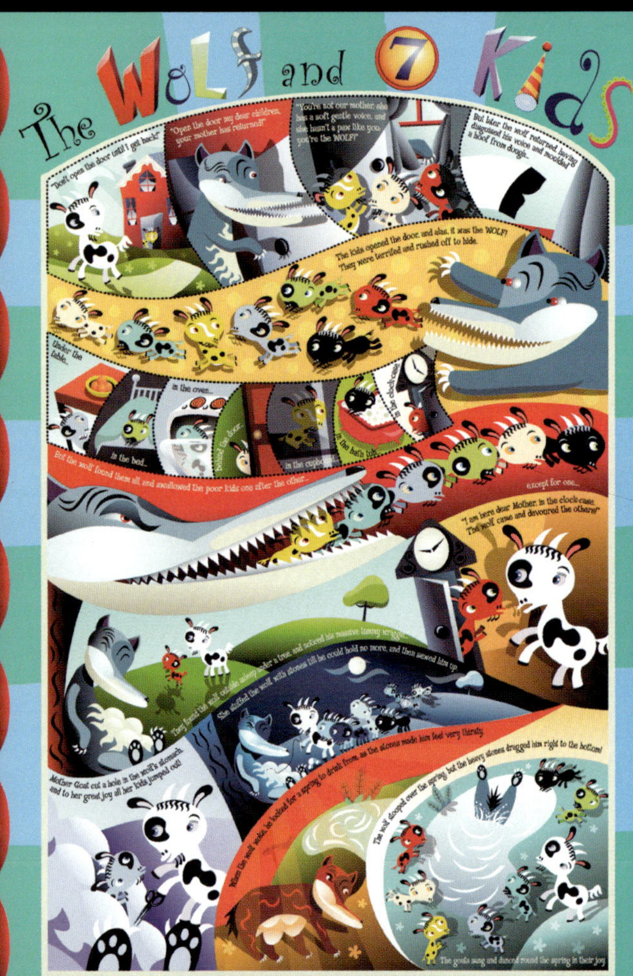

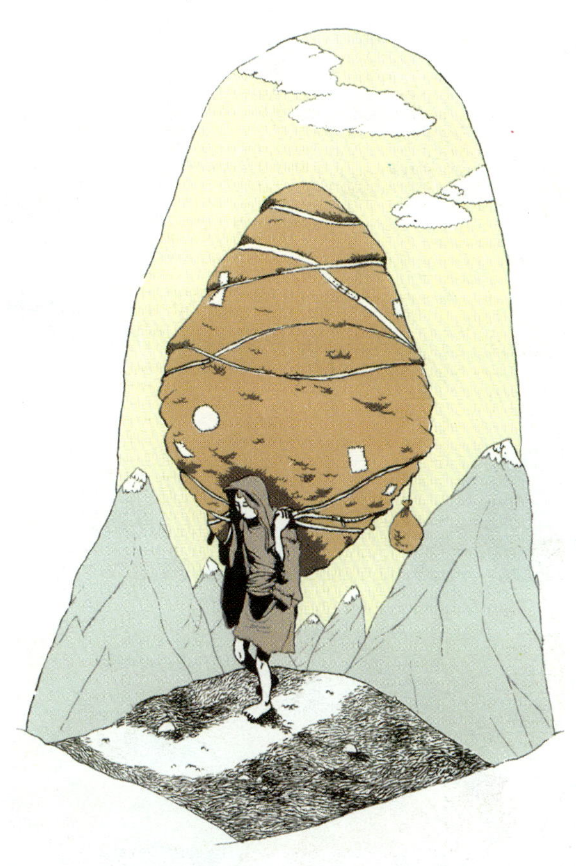

left: SHARON TANCREDI : s.tancredi@btintement.com
Instructor Geoff Grandfield, Middlesex University, London

above: LUKE THOMAS : luke_thomas85@hotmail.com
Instructor Tom Garrett, Minneapolis College of Art & Design, Minnesota

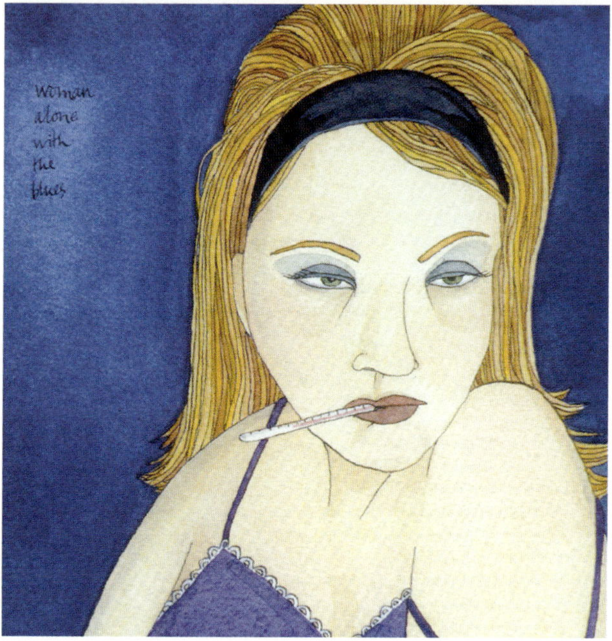

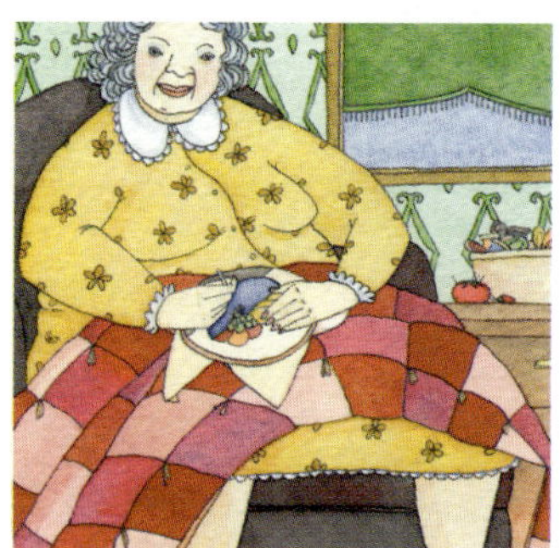

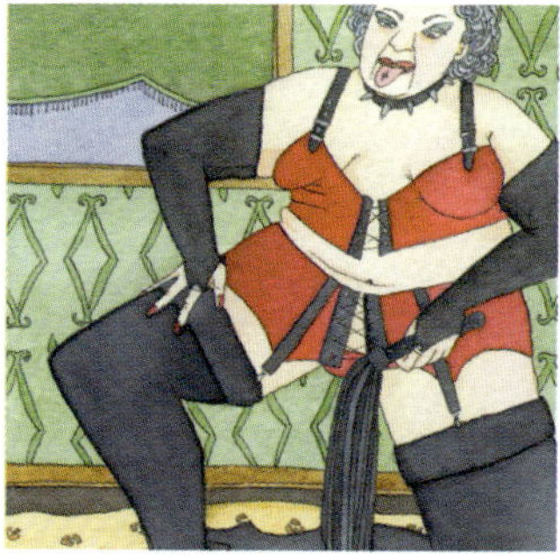

DAVEY THOMPSON : daveythompson@hotmail.com
Instructor Riccardo Stampatori, Sheridan College, Toronto, Canada

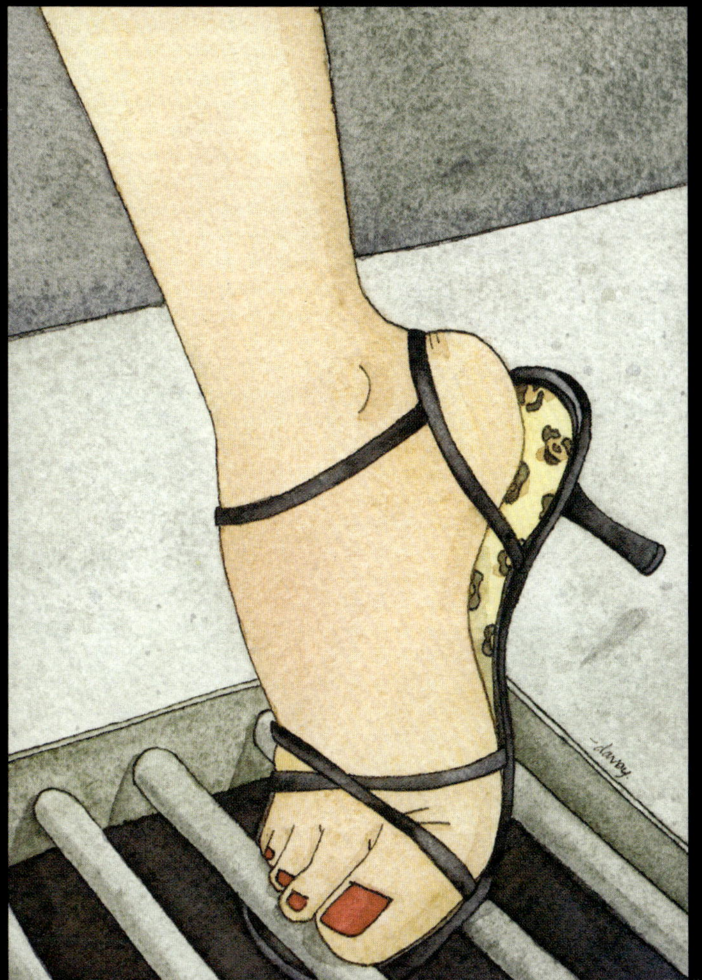

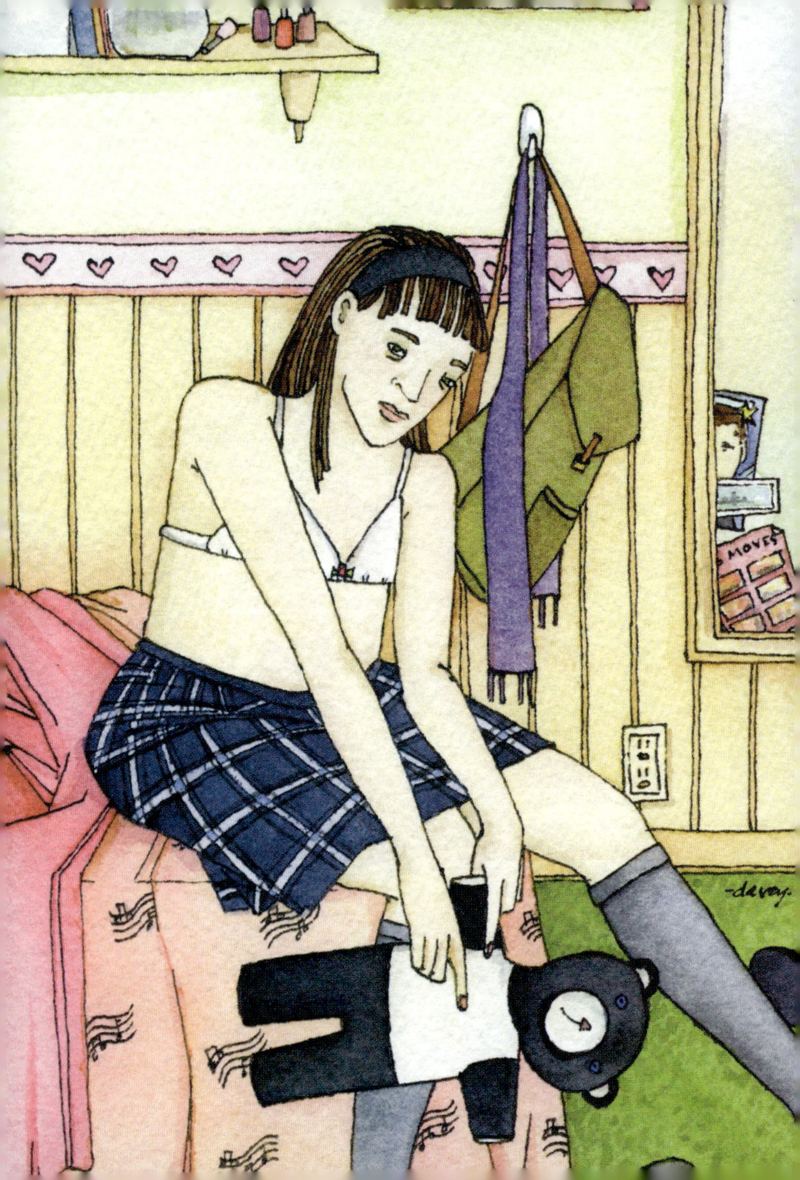

MOVES
-davey.

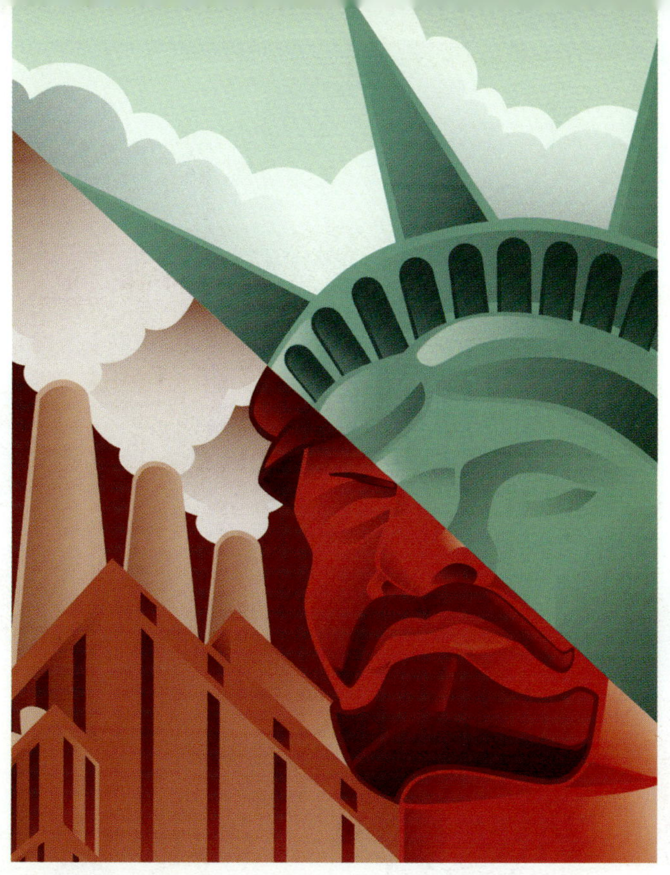

left: DAVEY THOMPSON : daveythompson@hotmail.com
Instructor Riccardo Stampatori, Sheridan College, Toronto, Canada

above: JOHN W. TOMAC : john@johnwtomaqc.com
Instructor Bill Finewood, Rochester Institute of Technology, New York

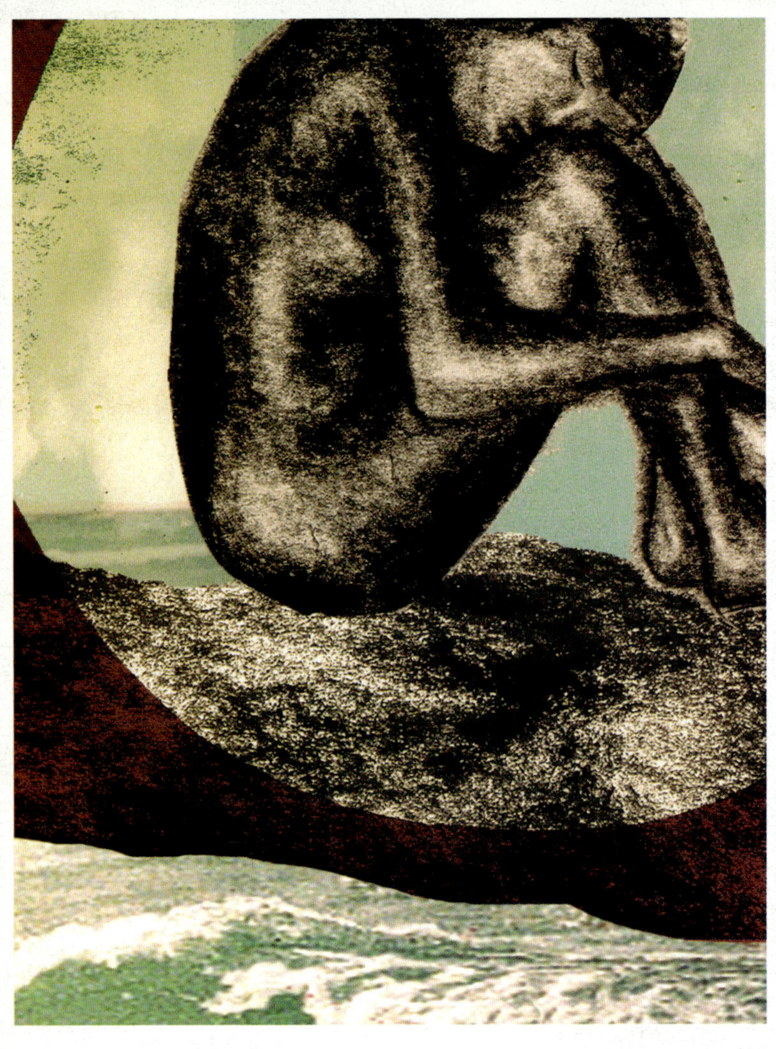

ANTHONY TREMMAGLIA : tremmaglia@hotmail.com

Instructor Tom Brown, Sheridan College, Toronto

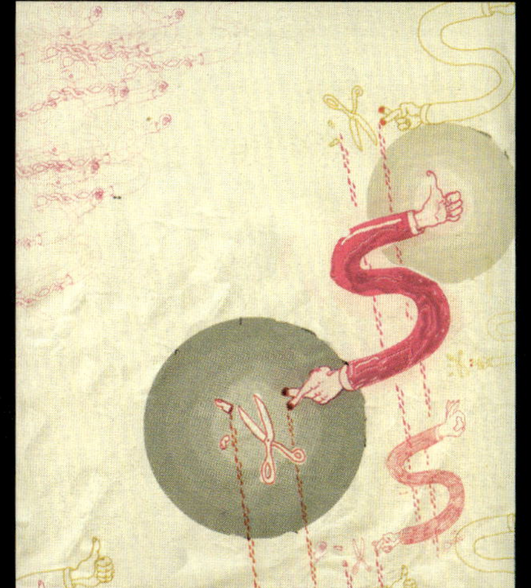

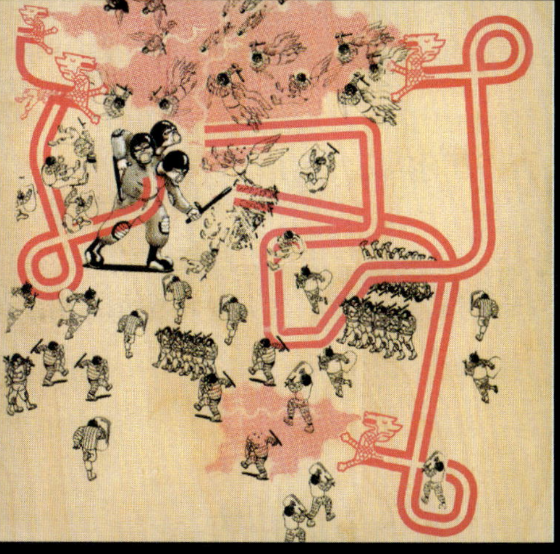

YAREK WASZUL : foonk@rogers.com

Instructor Paul Dallas, Ontario College of Art + Design, Toronto, Canada

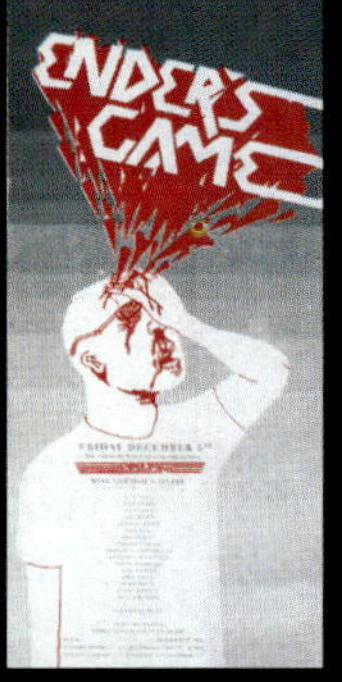

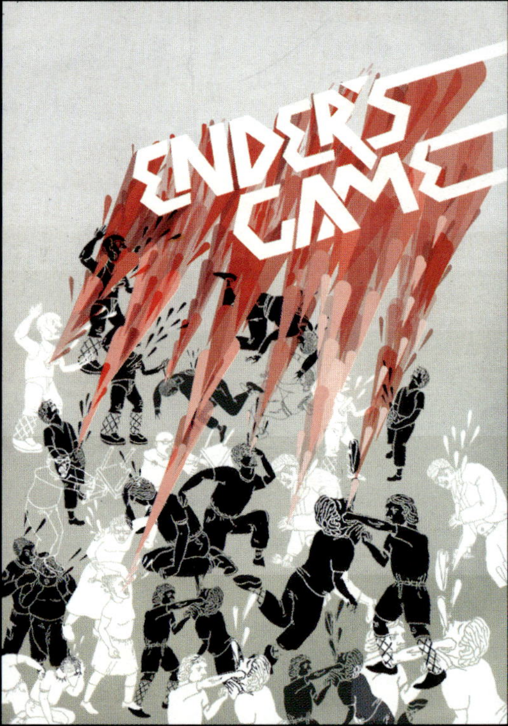

ENDER'S GAME
FRIDAY DECEMBER 5TH

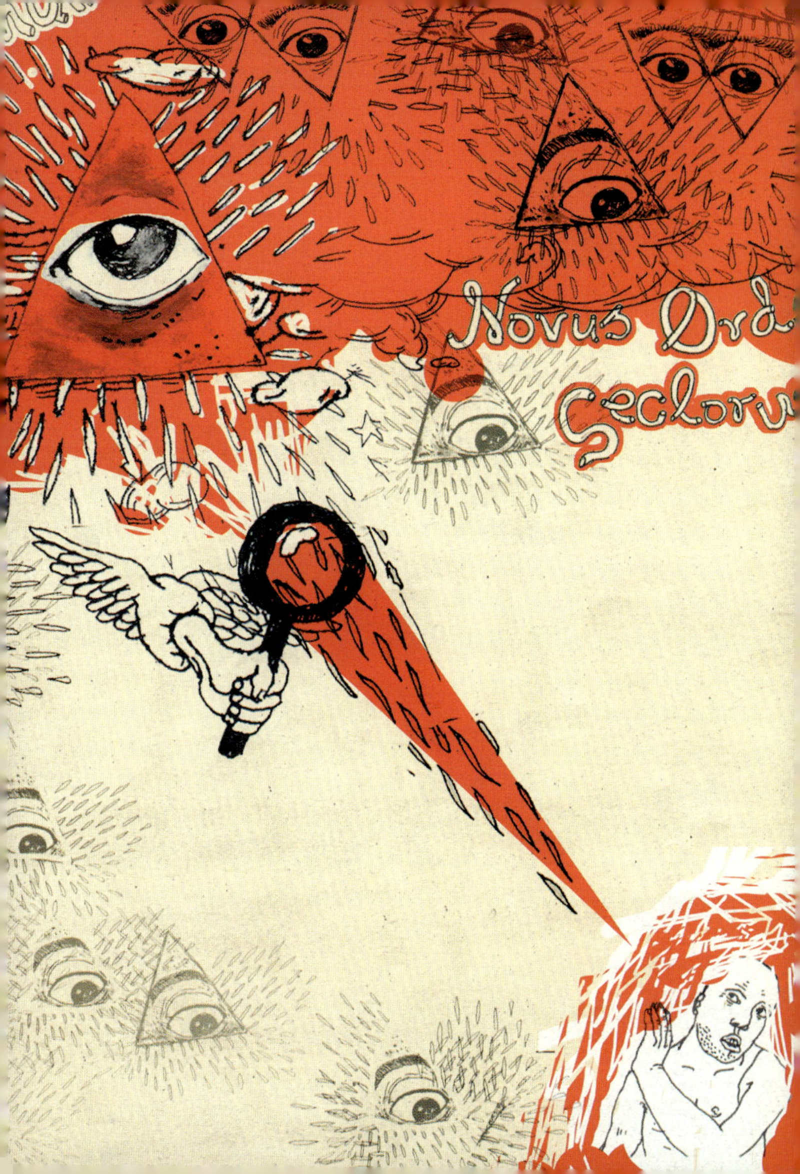
Novus Ord
Seclorum

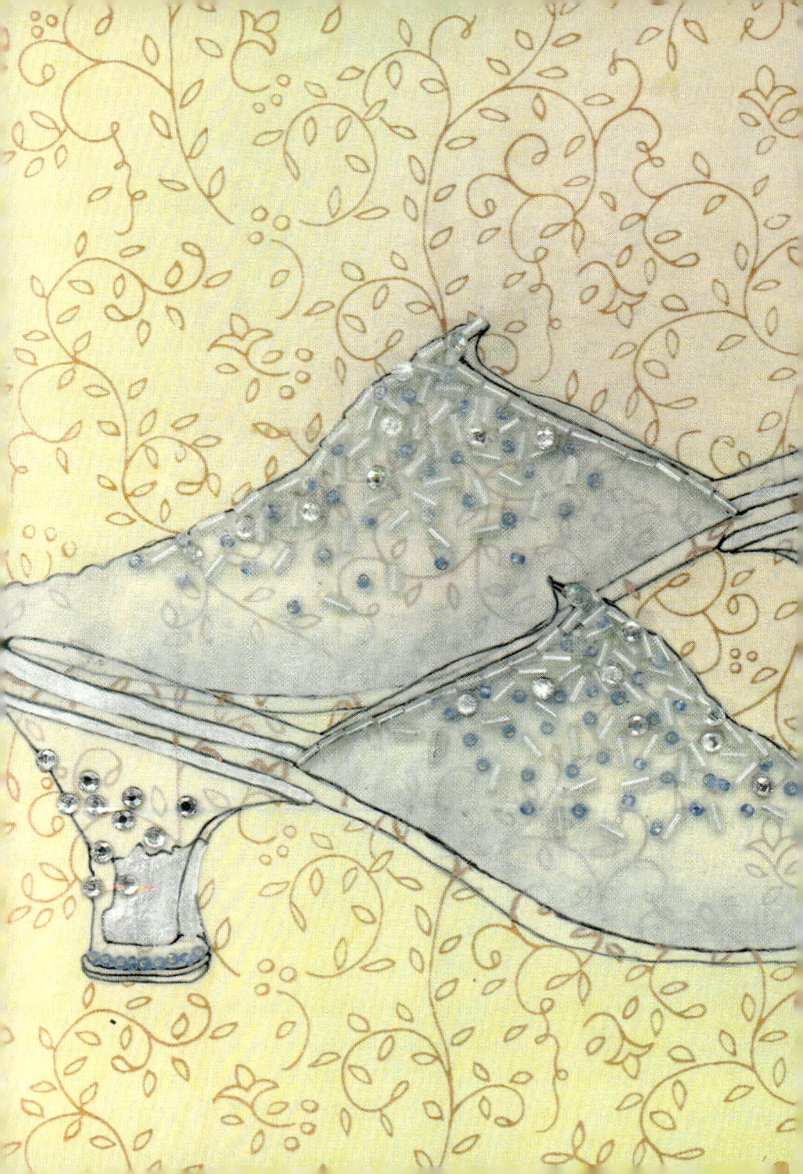

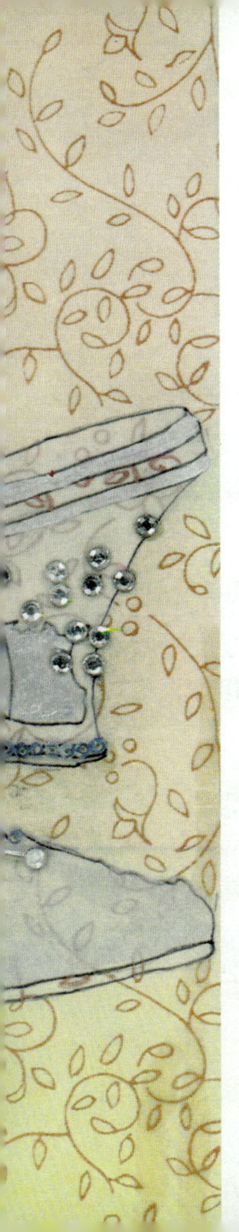

SARA WATERS : waterrose398@yahoo.com

Instructor Tom Garrett, Minneapolis College of Art & Design, Minnesota

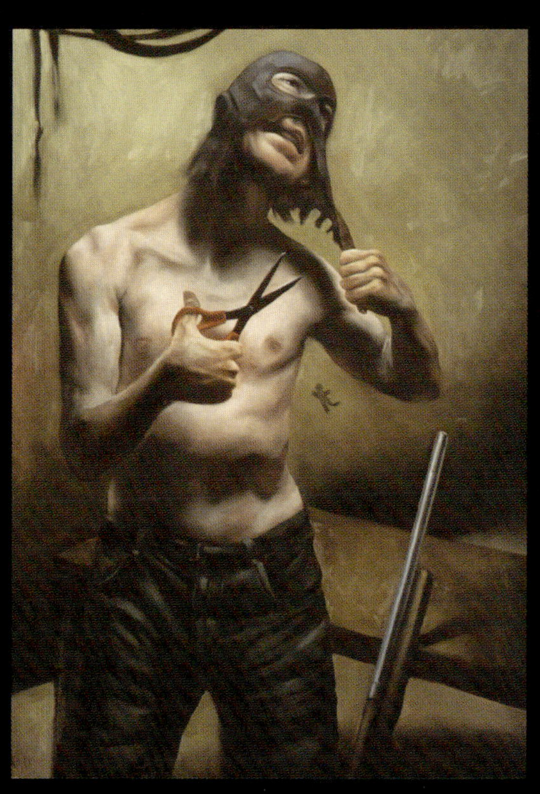

SAM WEBER : sam@sampaints.com

Instructor Marshall Arisman, School of Visual Arts, New York

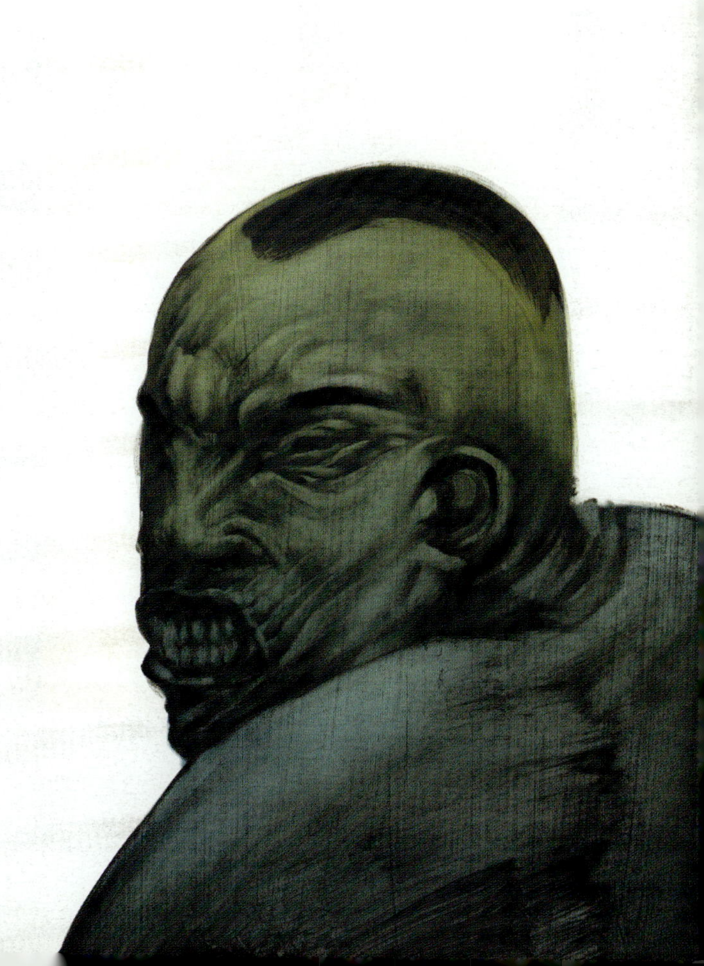

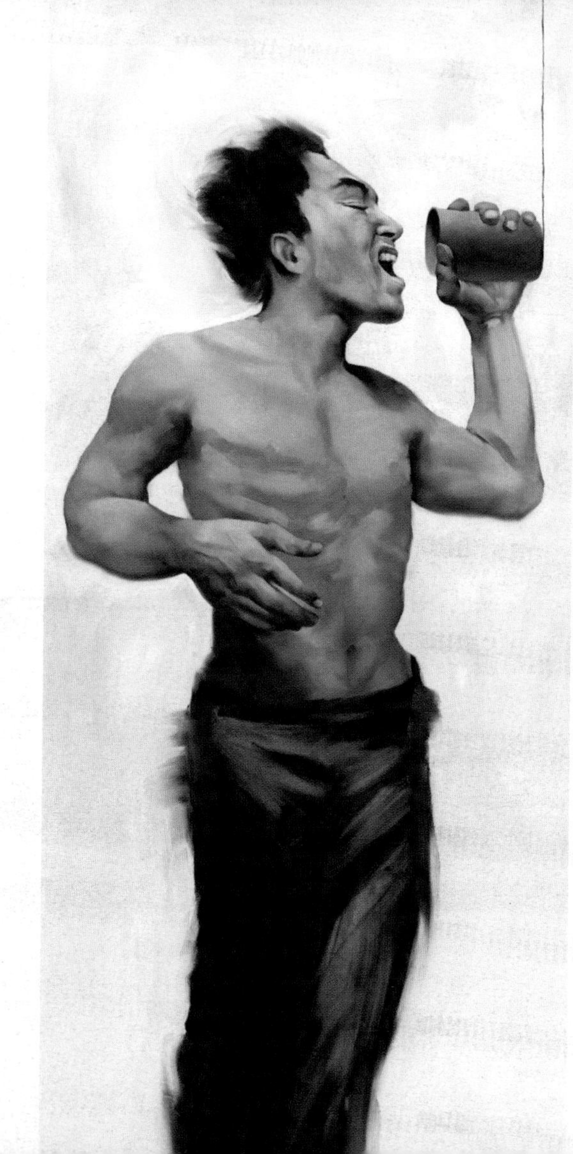

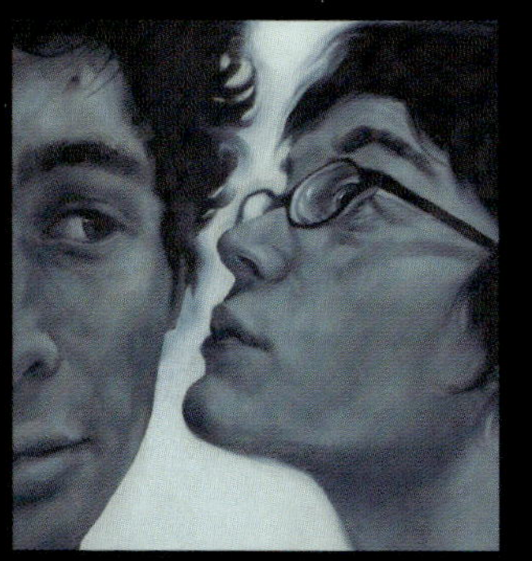

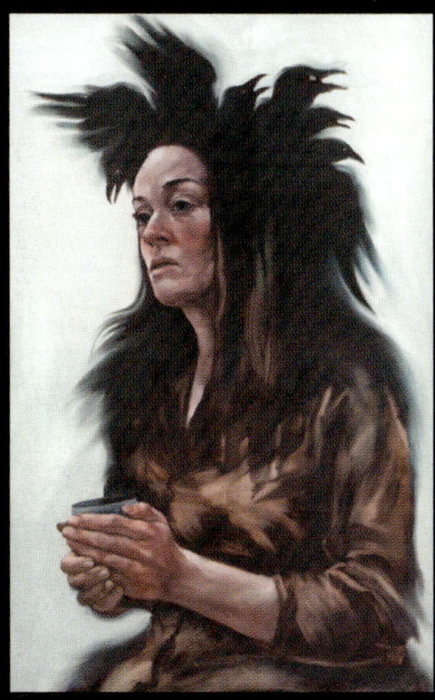

SAM WEBER : sam@sampaints.com
Instructor Marshall Arisman, School of Visual Arts, New York

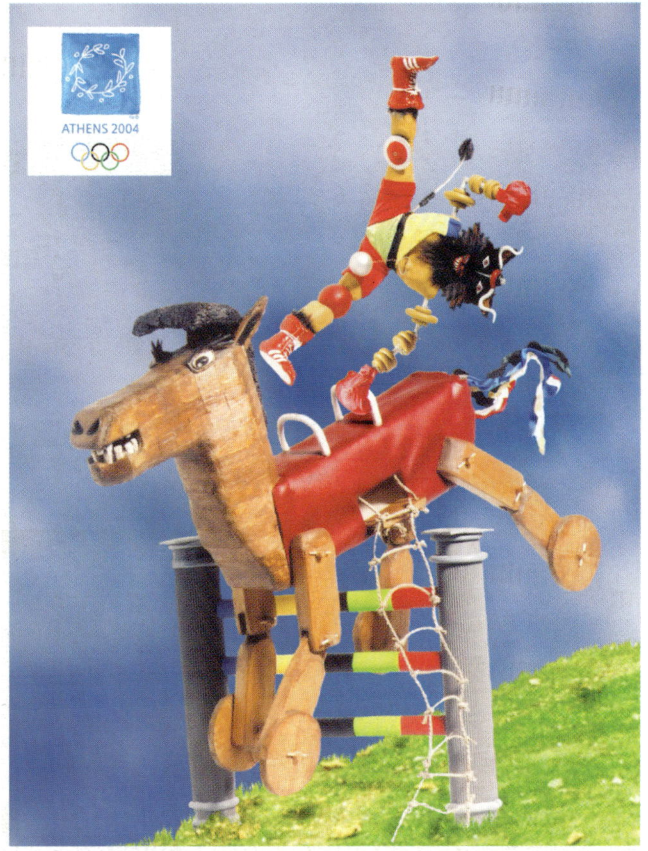

DEAN WILLIAMS : r.williamst51@ntlworld.com
Instructor Andrew Selby, Loughborough University, Leicestershire, United Kingdom

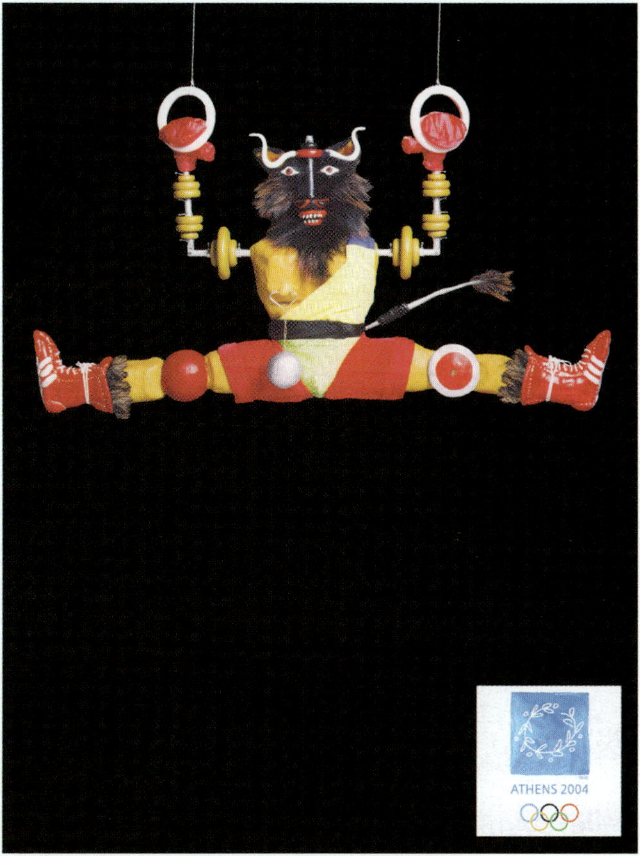

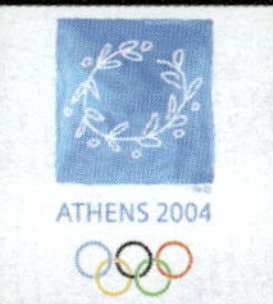
ATHENS 2004